A PASSION IN SIX DAYS
DOWNCHILD

For Ian McDiarmid

By the same author

Stage Plays

Cheek
No One Was Saved
Alpha Alpha
Edward, The Final Days
Stripwell
Claw
The Love of a Good Man
Fair Slaughter
That Good Between Us
The Hang of the Gaol
The Loud Boy's Life
Birth on a Hard Shoulder
Crimes in Hot Countries
No End of Blame
Victory

TV Plays

Cows
Mutinies
Prowling Offensive
Conrod
Heroes of Labour
Russia
All Bleeding
Heaven
Pity in History

Radio Plays

One Afternoon on the 63rd Level of the North Face
*   of the Pyramid of Cheops the Great*
Henry V in Two Parts
Herman with Millie and Mick
Scenes from an Execution

PLAYSCRIPT 108

A PASSION IN SIX DAYS

DOWNCHILD

Howard Barker

JOHN CALDER · LONDON
RIVERRUN PRESS · NEW YORK

First published in Great Britain, 1985, by
John Calder (Publishers) Limited
18 Brewer Street London W1R 4AS

and in the United States of America, 1985, by
Riverrun Press Inc
175 Fifth Avenue New York NY 10010

British Library Cataloguing in Publication Data

Barker, Howard
    A passion in six days; Downchild—(Playscript; 108)
    I. Title II. Barker, Howard. Downchild
    822'.914 PR6052.A6485

ISBN 0-7145-3985-6

Library of Congress Catalog No. 84-71907

Typeset 9/10 pt Press Roman by Gilbert Composing Services,
Leighton Buzzard, Bedfordshire.
Printed in Great Britain by Hillman Printers (Frome) Limited, Somerset

A Passion in Six Days

A PASSION IN SIX DAYS was first performed at the Crucible
Theatre, Sheffield, on 7th October, 1983, with the following cast:

RAYMOND TOYNBEE	Christopher Wilkinson
BRIAN GLINT	David Hargreaves
NIGEL PROUD	Toby Salaman
MONICA BOAKES	Lois Baxter
ERIC COIN	George Selway
STEPHEN FENTON	Jeffrey Chiswick
HARRY GAUKROGER	Harold Innocent
RAY SHAARD	Michael Irving
MALCOLM ARDSTOCK	Phil Whitchurch
JOHN AXT	Peter Wight
ANNIE AXT	Sian Thomas
SHADE	Jack Sprat
ANGELA BOYS	Joan Campion
PARRY	Michael Irving
KETCH	Jeffrey Chiswick
EMILY DRUM	Eliza Hunt
ELAINE TOYNBEE	Diana Berriman
LOUISE	Joan Campion
FRANK	George Selway
ALAN DEASY	Henry Stamper
LORD ISTED	Sebastian Shaw
SIR ROGER CLAXTON	Alec Linstead

CHORUS ⎫
ABSOLUTES ⎬ Mr Sprat's 21st Century Popular Motets
TECHNICIANS ⎬
WAITERS ⎭

Designed by   Roger Glossop
Directed by   Michael Boyd

ACT ONE

Scene One

A beach at night, the CHORUS, *almost at a whisper, sing 'The Curse of Debate'. As they raise the volume, an* OLD MAN *approaches the water's edge, undressed to swim.*

CHORUS.   **The Curse of Debate**

> Now you must concentrate,
> The level of debate
> Will test your ed–u–cation,
>
> Can you be ethical,
> Follow the technical,
> Without an ex–plan–ation?
>
> Please keep your mind alert,
> Tuck in your blouse or shirt,
> And do not spoil the ten–sion,
>
> When ideas that are bent
> And lives clearly mis–spent
> Claim too much a–ttention.
>
> Kindly retain your seat,
> The chairman won't repeat
> The rules of Con–ference,
>
> With your intellect
> You will of course detect
> The true things from the non–sense.
>
> Kindly ignore all lies
> And turn blind eyes
> To con–tra–dictions,
>
> Don't be offended by
> The great illumini
> Indulging futile fric–tions.

Lastly, do not expect too much
Of poor old human stuff
Which has not got your powers,

They want to save the state
But this entire debate
Will only last three ho–urs.

THIS IS THE DREAMING CITY
OF HOPE AND PAIN AND PITY
FORGIVE THEM THEIR ILL–USIONS,

ARE THEY FIT TO GOVERN,
ARE THEY LOOKING SLOVEN
ARE THEY GUILTY OF COLL–USIONS?

GAUKROGER. 'Ullo, Sea. It's me. 'arry Gaukroger. Down the pebbles
for me annual dip. Total immersion eight foot from the outfall
sewer. Shed me crust of dirty dealing, step out in sepulchral
whiteness, beaded from the elemental wash. 'ARRY GAUKROGER,
LISTEN TO 'ARRY. WHAT A FIGHTER, FORTY YEARS A
MEMBER, REVERENCE 'IS SACRIFICE! *(Pause)* Sea, listen. I
come 'ere with a warning. The old cracked vessel rings. From the
stand, the measured cadence of authority. 'ARRY WHO? MEMBER
FOR WHERE? 'e came naked but for honour, 'is features carved
by life as granite by the moorland weather. *(Pause)* Sea, listen. I come
to make the call of unity. Forty years I 'ave been silent, growing in
obscurity like the vintage in the rack. I 'ave been indolent, I'll admit
to you, but in the crisis I will blow my cork and BRING TEARS TO
THEIR EYES WITH MY 'EARTFELT PLEA. 'ARRY GAUKROGER,
WHO SPOKE AT LAST AND BROUGHT 'EM TO THEIR SENSES!
(Pause) Sea. Finally. I shan't be back. Forty years I 'ave been 'ere.
Old rib cage battling the breakers, comic legs up the shingle. They
'ave disowned me. ME! Enough to make yer surge in fury, dash the
winders of the 'all with spray, tidal wave of indignation, I WOULD
UNDERSTAND YER. *(Pause)* Remember me . . . *(He drops his
towel, waddles into the water)*

CHORUS.   **Love Is Sensible**

Down on the pebbles
There are rebels
In the shelter
Of the helter-skelter
Oaths are sworn
Ideas are born
And marriages
Re–ne–go–tia–ted!

Where is the treason
In using reason
In the field of love
No subject is above
Clinical dissection
Dialectical correction
Freedom won't be
Frus–tra–ted!

A MAN *and a* WOMAN *appear walking along the beach, slowly, painfully.*

AXT. I am trying. I feel sick but I am trying.

ANNE. You are, I know . . . .

AXT. You can feel it, can you? My little conflict?

ANNIE. Not little, I know . . .

AXT. My struggle with clinging stuff.

ANNIE. I applaud you.

AXT. I'm not after applause.

ANNIE. Appreciate you, then. Difficult, I know. All the male possession stuff. Having and holding. I appreciate you. Struggling.

AXT. Trying. Always trying. Can you imagine not trying? I can sometimes. The tranquillity of it. Still waters.

ANNIE. Not tranquillity. Stagnation.

AXT. Stagnation, yes. I am trying but I think of you. Your arse in my fingers.

ANNIE. All right.

AXT. Your tits in my hands.

ANNIE. My flesh. Lent, not sold.

AXT. Given . . . .

ANNIE. Yes. Lent.

AXT. Trying . . .

ANNIE. My flesh. My bits.

AXT. Look—

ANNIE. What? What's the problem?

AXT. Thinking—

ANNIE. Imagining—

AXT. Imagining, yes—

ANNIE. Why?

AXT. Why imagine?

ANNIE. Yes.

AXT. PEOPLE DO IMAGINE, DON'T THEY?

ANNIE. Shouting again. Very simple—

AXT. I know, I know—

ANNIE. My body—

AXT. His hands. His mouth. Feel sick again—

ANNIE. YOU GOT TO OVERCOME THIS THING! *(Pause. He walks to the water's edge)*

AXT. Sea. Constant sea. Up the beach, frothing at the feet of miserable
　　couples arguing their life. Must find it funny. Laugh its maritime
　　laugh. The little crisis in the little life. Mollusc debates with mollusc.

ANNIE. We are taking the absurdity out of marriage.

AXT. Yup.

ANNIE. The torture. Taking it out. *(There is a cry from the water.)*

GAUKROGER. 'ELP!

ANNIE. *(Hearing nothing).* Now. Look at me.

AXT. I look at you.

ANNIE. You look at me and you think—

AXT. I desire that woman.

ANNIE. No.

AXT. No.

ANNIE. You think—

AXT. That woman is free.

ANNIE. Good.

GAUKROGER. 'ELP!

AXT. I wish to share an act of love with—

ANNIE. Good—

AXT. Lending and being lent, but not—

GAUKROGER. 'ELP!

AXT. Possessing—

ANNIE. Poison of possession—

AXT. Yup—

ANNIE. Good—

AXT. Her needs, not my rights—

ANNIE. His needs, not my rights—

AXT. Good—

GAUKROGER. 'ELP, 'ELP!

A figure rushes onto the stage, throwing off his clothes as he runs.

GLINT *(to them).* There's a geezer in the water, are you deaf?
　　(Another figure hurries down, dressed)

GAUKROGER. 'ELP!

SHAARD. Brian—steady, Brian—

GLINT *(Naked now).* I'm going in—

SHAARD. Watch 'im, Brian—

GLINT. I will do— *(He wades in)*

SHAARD. Don't let 'im pull you under—

GLINT. *(In the dark now).* COMING!

AXT. Who is it?

SHAARD. 'ow should I fucking know? TO YER RIGHT, BRIAN!

GAUKROGER. 'ELP!

AXT. I can't swim.

SHAARD. Night before the bloody conference, in the drink.

AXT. I can't swim, you see . . . .

SHAARD. Keep it out the bloody papers— TO YER RIGHT, BRIAN!

AXT. My father, I don't think, in his whole life, TAUGHT ME ONE
   USEFUL THING . . .
SHAARD. *(Wading out).* Over 'ere!

AXT *stands paralyzed with despair.* GAUKROGER *is dragged up the
beach by* GLINT *and* SHAARD.

GAUKROGER. Ele–ment–al murderer! *(He waves his fist at the sea)*
   I cheated yer! Try to tow me under you ol' bastard! NEVER SET
   FOOT IN YER AGAIN! NEVER!
SHAARD. Did you 'ave any clothes?
GAUKROGER. TRAITOR!

GLINT *ignores him, walks up the beach, starts drying himself roughly
with his trousers. He sees* ANNIE *looking at him.*

GLINT. Don't look at me like that, you'll make me blush . . . *(She turns
away.* SHAARD *comes up)*
SHAARD. It's the member for Sham Hammerton. Needn't 'ave
   bothered, yer can't sink with a gutful of liquor.
GAUKROGER. HARRY GAUKROGER FLOATS.
GLINT. Specific gravity of whisky . . .
GAUKROGER. *(Still addressing the sea).* 'E FLOATS . . . !

GLINT *and* SHAARD *walk off up the beach.*

ANNIE. Hard and naked . . . shone with water . . . marble white man . . .
GAUKROGER. *(Seeing Axt).* What the 'ell . . .
AXT. Harry . . . Christ . . .
GAUKROGER. Yer nearly made it . . .
AXT. It's not the way I'd choose to have you out.
GAUKROGER. Congratulate me, then! CONGRATULATE ME ON
   RETAINING MY SEAT DESPITE THE OPPOSITION!
AXT. I do . . .
GAUKROGER. Fuck it, Ann, I saw the lights go, I was in the arms of
   death . . .
ANNIE. Yer too old to swim.
GAUKROGER. Cramp. The old iron in the hip. Like I was in a band of
   steel. Pulling. Down goes 'arry, down among the boss-eyed sea bass. 'oh
   pulled me out? The bugger stuck 'is elbow in between me legs.
AXT. Brian Glint. *(Pause)*
GAUKROGER. Brian Glint? *(He swells)* BRIAN GLINT?
AXT. Down the pebbles very proud, casting his two-tone suit, and
   plunge! A knot of muscularity in the servile water, which cleaves for
   him . . . BRIAN GLINT. *(ANNIE looks at him)* He buys silk shirts.
   The labels have his name in, woven like a schoolboy. He loves good
   clothes, and things caressing him . . . BRIAN GLINT . . .
ANNIE. What's up.

GAUKROGER. I'll buy 'im a brandy . . .

ANNIE. Careful, Harry . . .

GAUKROGER. No, be my witness, I will buy 'im a brandy. *(He turns, ecstatically)* Christ, it's good to be alive, 'ULLO, WORLD! I was spared to make my speech. Agents of the loony left 'ad brainwashed the mackerel but I fought back. Something greater than me was at work—THE SPIRIT OF DEMOCRACY.

ANNIE. What speech is this, Harry?

GAUKROGER. You'll 'ear.

ANNIE. You don't make speeches.

GAUKROGER. Correction. I 'ave not made speeches—YET. *(He starts moving up the beach, stops)* Brian Glint. *(Pause)* The beginning of a great political relationship. The old, the knowledgeable, and the young instinctive, a bond forged in the ocean. I will stand be'ind 'is throne and whisper the advice of forty years of labourism, and on my funeral 'e will deliver an oration which will make the eyes of 'ardened newsmen flush like bog pans. We shall be father and son.

ANNIE. You have a son already.

GAUKROGER. I 'ave a son, but 'e's an estate agent. 'is mother took the soul out of 'im and put a tin whistle there instead. He doesn't speak, 'e peeps. No, I was made to sire lifeguards. *(He moves on)* Brian Glint . . . I shall stick my ol' grey 'ead against 'is shoulder, and nudge 'im through the gates of 'istory . . . *(He waddles away. ANNIE looks at AXT)*

ANNIE. What? *(He does not reply)* One of your dark things coming over? *(Pause)* I can taste it. Off your tense body like an acrid sweat. *(Pause. She extends a hand)* Let's watch world horrors in the guest lounge. *(He ignores her)* People under bombs. Blood and rubble. Gets your mood down. Dwarfs it—*(He shakes his head)* Oh, what! *(Pause)* I do think, if we are to carry on, you must expose more. I know you try. You do try, but—I MEAN EXPRESS IT AND IT CAN BE DISCUSSED. *(Pause. He is staring down at the ground)*

I Saw Him Naked

ANNIE.   Was it the way I looked at him
           When he was naked on the pebbles,
           Very white, upright, and very strong?
           He was dark voiced in the dark night,
           Altogether male stereotype,
           But I liked it, is that so very wrong?

AXT.   He is an opportunist bastard,
           A careerist with no honour
           Cynically manipulating life,
           How do you think I feel to see him
           Prancing like a pigeon
           Under the fascinated gloating of my wife?

ANNIE. A woman can appreciate a man
      As a pysical creation,
      Where exactly is the sin in that?
      When I first met you you had pictures
      Of girls' arses and split beavers
      On every door and cupboard of the flat.

AXT. I can't make sense of my feelings
      But I would die if you had dealings
      With a traitor to the left like Brian Glint;
      I know the body, a contraption,
      For finding satisfaction
      But anyone who touches him's a bint.

ANNIE. Amazing. When you let go. The things you can come out with. Staggers me.

AXT. Yes.

ANNIE. The words. The oppression in the words.

AXT. Go home then!

ANNIE. Yes, alright, I will. *(She exits)*

AXT. Annie!

TOYNBEE *and* ELAINE *enter.*

TOYNBEE. I envy people who govern during wars. It is simplicity itself. The test of a statesman is what he can achieve in peace. To change with consent—*(The woman whistles the dog)* with consent—

ELAINE. He is going near those—*(She whistles again)*

TOYNBEE.—is the supreme gift of the great man to the people, the highest moment of a political culture—

ELAINE. Here!

TOYNBEE. I dread this conference, Elaine.

ELAINE. You dread them all.

TOYNBEE. No . . .

ELAINE. 'The little and the vicious reign for seven days', your words.

TOYNBEE. The ritual I abhor, and yet—

ELAINE. Spewings of dry little brains. The half-educated flinging epithets rather crudely wrought. Rehearsed abuse. You sit with hatred running down your face, cocked head like a man in stocks as some contorted—ugh—I can't go on, all the loathing on the floor, awash like the submerged deck of a refuse barge . . . *(The dog comes)* Good boy, good boy!

TOYNBEE. It is democracy.

ELAINE. Stay away from nasty bins—

TOYNBEE. The leader submits, not only to the correction, but also to the ill-will of his subordinates.

ELAINE. Imagine a flower-garden outside Oxford—

TOYNBEE. He is wounded only by the knowledge of his own error—

ELAINE. Night stocks and delphiniums—

TOYNBEE. Not by the degree of antagonism he provokes—

ELAINE. And honeysuckle sweet as nakedness on the still air . . .

TOYNBEE. Burke. On the Constitution and the Governors. Given at Holborn, 1811.

ELAINE. Very good. There are spiteful mongrels on this beach. And tin cans left to cut his pads. He hates dirt and masses. Even empty this beach smells of masses, like a train carriage, is stained where heads and arses lay basking in the common sun . . .

A voice comes from the darkness.

ARDSTOCK. Raymond? Raymond? *(The dog begins barking ferociously)* Fuckin' 'ell—

ELAINE. Down, down, Ruff—

ARDSTOCK. *(Mock Humour).* IT'S ONLY ME YER STUPID DOG! *(It growls)* Never liked me, has it? Never has.

ELAINE. Your smell.

ARDSTOCK. I do my best.

ELAINE. Desperate best, you do.

ARDSTOCK. I do, and yet—

ELAINE. Spaniels aren't rational, bribable; or compassionate. I love them.

TOYNBEE. What is it, Malcolm?

ARDSTOCK. I hope I'm not intruding—

ELAINE. He always says that, don't you?

ARDSTOCK. Do I?

ELAINE. Hope I'm not intruding . . .

ARDSTOCK. I must cut it out.

ELAINE. Of course you are intruding.

ARDSTOCK. *(Sarcastically).* Sacred intercourse of man and wife?

ELAINE. What would you know about that?

ARDSTOCK. Not a great, deal, unfortunately.

TOYNBEE. Buck up, Malcolm—

ELAINE. *(To* ARDSTOCK). Do you realize you talk in stock phrases?

ARDSTOCK. Do I? I'm not a poet—

ELAINE. No, you're not, You're not sorry at all—

TOYNBEE. CAN WE JUST GET ON?

ELAINE. *(Drifting away).* He's not sorry at all. Why did he say that? Why does everybody tell lies?

ARDSTOCK. *(To* TOYNBEE, *darkly).* 468.

TOYNBEE. What about it?

ARDSTOCK. We've lost the seamen.

TOYNBEE. *(Shocked).* How?

ARDSTOCK. Ask Reg.

TOYNBEE. I will ask Reg. Now I'm asking you.

ARDSTOCK. Someone's been getting at his executive—

TOYNBEE. HE TOLD ME THE EXECUTIVE WAS IN HIS POCKET.

ARDSTOCK. I know he did, he told me, too—

TOYNBEE *(barks)*. I CAN'T TAKE ANY MORE OF THIS!
ARDSTOCK. It'll still carry, Raymond—
TOYNBEE. SICK AND TIRED OF PEOPLE NOT DELIVERING
   WHAT THEY—
ARDSTOCK. *(Seeing people approach)*. Shuddup—
TOYNBEE. ENDLESS WRITHING AND—
ARDSTOCK. Shuddup, will yer!

A group of young conference delegates appears walking along the beach.

Eat Your Defeats

ABSOLUTES. Frank an' Mick an' Ralph an' Tony,
      Susan, Ali–son an' Ro–ny,
      Stayin' at the Dolphin B an' B,
      Nine solid months of organizin',
      Jumble sales an' caucusisin',
      To carry resolution ninety-three,

      Shovin' things through letter box flaps,
      Climbin' vandalized blocks of flats,
      Talkin' to ol' geezers through the door,
      Anyone who wants to transform
      Shouldn't look up to the platform,
      Democracy is somethin' you find on the floor!

      Frank an' Mick an' Ralph an' Tony,
      Susan, Ali–son an' Ro–ny,
      Stayin' at the Dolphin B an' B,
      Every setback is instruction
      To be studied in discussion,
      Socialism 'as its tides just like the sea . . .

RONY. *(seeing* TOYNBEE). Comrades! We are not alone—
MALCOLM/ALISON. *(Chanting)*. It's Ray–mond, it's Ray–mond—
RONY. In our desire to rinse the urban squalor—
MALCOLM/ALISON. It's Ray–mond, it's Ray–mond—
RONY. From our eyes and ears—
MALCOLM/ALISON. GET – BACK – TO – THE – 'OSPITAL!
RONY. *(Mocking)*. I may not agree with what you say—
MALCOLM/ALISON. It's Ray–mond, it's Ray–mond—
RONY. But by God—
MALCOLM/ALISON. It's Ray–mond, it's Ray–mond—
RONY. I will defend your right to say it!
MALCOLM/ALISON/RALPH. GET – BACK – TO – THE –
   'OSPITAL! *(They fall about laughing)*.

TOYNBEE. I believe this is a public place—of some considerable
  dimensions—I wonder if you would be—kind enough—to chant
  your slogans—in another part of the beach—
MICK. This isn't the House of Commons, you are permitted to speak
  English as it is popularly understood—
ARDSTOCK. Fuck off or I will bust yer face— *(The militants cheer)*
TONY. The two tongues of the leadership—fusty an' fisty—
TOYNBEE. I do not think it is too much to ask, even of opponents
  as rabid with the infection of totalitarianism as—*(They cheer)* Yes,
  totalitarianism—as you are—
ARDSTOCK. I don't think this is—
TOYNBEE. As contemptuous of tolerance—and as—
ARDSTOCK. Going to get us very—
TOYNBEE. Inveterately hostile—*(They cheer)* to the traditions of this
  party—
ARDSTOCK. Is it?
TOYNBEE. That a man may walk with his dog—
RONY. What about your wife?
TOYNBEE. On a summer evening—
RONY. Dog first, wife after—
TOYNBEE. *(Rising temper).* Without encountering the inane and
  mindless—
ABSOLUTES. Oh, Ray—mond, oh, Ray—mond—
TOYNBEE. DO YOU WONDER WE ARE NOT WINNING ELECTIONS!
ARDSTOCK. Raymond, I think—
TOYNBEE. No, you do not wonder because you do not actually
  believe in them! You no more believe in the principles of democracy—
ABSOLUTES. Oh Raymond, Oh Raymond . . .
TOYNBEE. Than you would believe the rules of cricket . . . WHO
  COULD PLAY CRICKET WITH YOU!
ABSOLUTES. Get back to the hospital!
TOYNBEE. You are a most monstrous ex—exrescence—*(They cheer)* Yes.
  excrescence, on the body of this party. (ARDSTOCK *moves towards
  them)* Malcolm—
ABSOLUTES. C.I.A.! C.I.A.!
TOYNBEE. MALCOLM!
ABSOLUTES. *(Chanting).* The violence of the leadership . . . !
ARDSTOCK. You little bastard, I'll break your neck!
ABSOLUTES. The violence of the leadership . . . !

ARDSTOCK *pushes them off violently. He does not reappear. Pause.*

ELAINE. I want to be fucked in a dark garden . . .
TOYNBEE. By whom?
ELAINE. An intellectual who has suffered for his goodness. Want
  him naked and uneasy in the perfect grass. White haired in the
  moonlight, old as me . . .
  They drift away.

Scene Two

The Hotel Louise. A boarding house.

CHORUS. Harry Gaukroger requires an intimate hotel,
    A democrat he hates all waiters and the smell
    Of stiff dress.

    He's had a long demanding day
    He likes to go home quietly and have away
    His hostess

    For the honeymooners' bedroom he reserves
    All his powers, this is the comrade who deserves
    His prowess

    Thirty years now he has booked in the Louise
    They've grown old together but their knees
    Still tremble

    Harry, the sheets are already folded down
    For the best fringe meeting in the town . . .

GAUKROGER. Frank! Run us a bath. I'm half dead!
LOUISE. What?
GAUKROGER. How old am I? How old am I?
LOUISE. Sixty-three.
GAUKROGER. Sixty-three. SIXTY-THREE, and what? I am dragging
    kids out of the water . . .
FRANK. *(Aghast)*. Dragging kids out of—
GAUKROGER. 'e struggled, 'e panicked, it was all I could do to 'old
    'im, 'e groins me, 'e winds me, 'e puts 'is barmy fingers round me
    throat, I'M SAVIN' YER, DON'T STRUGGLE, but you can't
    reason with a madman, so I cuffed 'im, subdued 'im with a single,
    masterful blow to the throat—
FRANK. The throat?
GUAKROGER. Yes, the throat, why not the throat, and swum with 'im
    limp as cod onto the shingle, laid 'im down and started respiration, 'e
    looks, 'is eyes open, an' fixing mine 'e says, 'my saviour, my saviour.'
    It was Brian Glint. Don't breathe a word of this.
FRANK. Brian Glint . . . ?
GAUKROGER. He swims, apparently, but not well. 'My saviour, my
    saviour . . .' Is the bath 'ot?
FRANK. *(affected)*. Brian Glint . . .
GAUKROGER. The bath, Frank.
FRANK. *(Recalled)*. Right away! *(He hurries out)*
LOUISE. You astonishin' old bugger . . .
GAUKROGER. No man knows what he is capable of until the test . . .
    show us yer tits . . . *(He embraces her)*

LOUISE. Later—

GAUKROGER. Show us, I love 'em— *(He caresses her)* 'ave yer missed me?

LOUISE. I survived—

GAUKROGER. *(Moved).* Oh, my . . . oh, my—

LOUISE. He goes out to the market, seven o'clock, regular—

GAUKROGER. Bless 'im, bring us breakfast in bed—

LOUISE. Boiled egg?

GAUKROGER. And two slices of—bloody 'ell, Lou, I shan't sleep tonight, come tonight, come—

LOUISE. How can I?

GAUKROGER. Something—

LOUISE. What—

GAUKROGER. Anything—

LOUISE. Oh, bloody—

GAUKROGER. I'll call down from the bathroom—

LOUISE. What for?

GAUKROGER. Talc.

LOUISE. Have to be quick—

GAUKROGER. I am quick, just to 'ave you—touch the—

LOUISE. All right, you shout—*(She goes out)*

FRANK. *(Entering).* 'ot, deep, and steaming . . .

GAUKROGER. I long for it.

FRANK. The way I see socialism—

GAUKROGER. Linen sheets, I'ope? None of yer nylon rubbish?

FRANK. Same as ever.

GAUKROGER. I can't sleep in nylon. I itch. Get rashes.

FRANK. I see it as advancing like a restless tide. So gradual as to be imperceptible, as on a beach the sleeping tripper wakes to find his knees submerged . . .

GAUKROGER. I'll go up, then.

FRANK. There are many socialisms, as there are many plants in the garden, exotic, plain, floribunda, and so on, but they thrust their roots into the common soil . . .

GAUKROGER. Are you pissed, Frank? (FRANK *looks up*).

FRANK. What time do you want breakfast?

GAUKROGER. Conference kicks off at 'alf past nine. I'll 'ave it up in my room.

FRANK. I shan't see you, then. I go out for the veg at—

GAUKROGER. Pity.

FRANK. Carry on this discussion in the evening.

GAUKROGER. Why not?

FRANK. I'd like that. I see socialism as—

GAUKROGER. Better get up. 'ave the bathroom swamped otherwise.

FRANK. Goo' night.

GAUKROGER. Sleep tight. *(He starts to leave)*.

FRANK. Harry.

GAUKROGER. Yup?

FRANK. 'onoured to have you, at Hotel Louise.
GAUKROGER. Appreciate the welcome.
FRANK. Always.
GAUKROGER. Cheers, ol' son . . .

HE goes out. LOUISE enters. FRANK shakes his head.

FRANK. Brian Glint! Goes and pulls out Brian Glint.
LOUISE. Pity.
FRANK. *(Appalled).* Sorry?
LOUISE. Pity
FRANK. There are many shades within the spectrum of the party—
   (A cry off)
LOUISE. I'll go—
FRANK. No, you sit and—
LOUISE. I'll go—
FRANK. What is it?
LOUISE. Forgot his talc.
FRANK. I'll get it—
LOUISE. No, I'm up now—
FRANK. No, I—
LOUISE. LOOK, HE DOESN'T WANT TO TALK SOCIALISM WITH
   YOU. *(Pause)* Talking socialism all day. Honour the guests . . .

She goes.

Scene Three

*The Gymnasium of the Imperial Hotel. GLINT enters, among the
shadows. He leans.*

Don't worry, he's not serious

GLINT. I would very much have liked to be a singer,
      In a club oozing from table lamp to lamp,
      My wicked eyes would catch out women during dinner,
      I'd perch on stools, wear jewels, and be a little camp;
      But in the car park after dark I'd bunch my knuckles,
      Roll up belt buckles and kick the eyeballs out of tramps . . .
      I would be the subject of journalistic speculation,
      How many kids I'd fathered would be gossip in the Sun,
      Duchesses would use my picture for masturbation,
      Lorry drivers cut their hair in imitation
      And lots of girls commit suicide if I died young . . .

PROUD. *(Entering).* You know what you need . . .
GLINT. I know what you think I need.

PROUD. A bit of unearned privilege.

GLINT. I think you got it all, Nigel.

PROUD. Three years at Cambridge. Scholarship boy. Little bit uneasy, snaps when teased. A bit of brawling in the quad. Breaks nose of toff. Kicks queer tutor in the W.H. Audens.

GLINT. Go on . . .

PROUD. Finds vacs difficult with proletarian dad. Declasse all over the place. Loses wicked temper, which becomes a charm. Climbs, exits, then rebukes. Hates privilege as only the privileged know how.

GLINT. I must say, Nigel, when I look at you, I don't see where the Socialism comes in.

PROUD. You mean the proletarianism. Not the same thing.

GLINT. Ask the workers.

PROUD. I prefer not to.

GLINT. I bet.

PROUD. Joke, silly.

GLINT. Liar.

PROUD. Joke, I said.

GLINT. What's Freud say about jokes, the—

PROUD. Somehow the spectacle of you invoking Freud is—

GLINT. Jokes are unconscious interventions of—

PROUD. You have never read Freud, so don't –

GLINT. You are such a little, shrivelled snob. A wizened, dessicated snob. With some yellow trickle in your veins. And an arse like the last prune in the packet. Don't make me loathe you or I shall get rough.

PROUD. Wear it like a decoration.

GLINT. Would you, by Christ—

PROUD. Loathed by the loathsome, first class with bar.

GLINT. *(Turning away).* Oh, fuck, I can't talk with a wit.

PROUD. Or like one, either.

GLINT. Get back to yer banker's stool, yer wheedling bugger . . .

PROUD. *(Looking at his watch).* Where is Monica?

GLINT. You did tell her, the gym?

PROUD. Eight o'clock, I said. The gym.

GLINT. You'd think she'd be here, working some inches off her arse.

PROUD. It's not a beauty contest, Brian, it's a conference—

GLINT. Speak for yourself—*(A woman enters)* You're ten minutes late, darling.

BOAKES. Why do we have to meet in the gym? There are ninety-seven rooms in the hotel, why the—

GLINT. Bugged.

BOAKES. *(Contemptuously).* Paranoia.

PROUD. I hate that word. I hate all words which are fashionable. I hate bugged. I hate paranoia, for that matter.

BOAKES. What's got into Nigel?

PROUD. There she goes again. Nothing's GOT INTO me. The language of the poly snack bar . . .

GLINT. It's where the party workers come from, Nigel, in case you
hadn't noticed. My CLP is full of doctors and not one of 'em can
bandage a finger. Mind you, they don't wear bras either, so it's
not all bad . . . *(A man enters)* Hello, Eric, decent bit of sole, was
it? The Liebfraumilch comes with the compliments of Sarsons,
have you noticed? Chateau Chlorine.

COIN. *(Coldly)*. About Raymond. *(He walks a little, hands in pockets,
stops, looks at them)* How long has he got?

BOAKES. The veins are dying. The capillaries. Like thread worms in
the sun.

COIN. Nigel?

PROUD. I spoke to the neurologist.

PROUD. I spoke to the neurologist. Progressive deterioration of the
brain cells due to blood starvation. Will make him do things. Be
embarrassing in restaurants. Make groundless accusations against his
wife. Lose the ability to distinguish between friends and foes.

COIN. So how long has he got? You're close to him, Brian, we're not.

I Kissed his Cheek

GLINT. I am as close to him as any killer to his victim,
　　Who may have been his lover, his disciple or his wife,
　　But on some dark, hot summer evening
　　Comes at him with a broken bottle or a knife;

　　I impress him with my manly way of standing,
　　Like an Epstein I occupy a block of space;
　　He looks at me and there is envy in his frailness
　　For the coal and iron and steel in my embrace.

　　Every leader from Jesus Christ to Fidel Castro
　　Knows the handshake is dishonest and the kiss is a disease,
　　It's the price the governor pays to be the governor,
　　When I'm the governor, you come in on your knees . . .

PROUD. It's not a hereditary monarchy, Brian.

COIN. Never mind Brian's—

PROUD. No, never mind, but I just say it anyway, the leadership is a
contest, open to all. I renounce nothing. I am in the running.

GLINT. As ever.

PROUD. As ever.

GLINT. Eighth time lucky.

BOAKES. Can we leave the leadership election until we have
dispensed with the leader?

PROUD. I make the point because—

COIN. I think we know why you—

PROUD. No, Eric, I'll finish if you don't mind, because if we allow
Brian to parade about in the mantle of the heir apparent we will

fall into his trap—

GLINT. What's my trap?

PROUD. Psychology.

GLINT. Never heard of it.

PROUD. We will—unconsciously—begin to see Brian as Brian wants himself to be seen. So I challenge any assumption. The art of politics—

BOAKES. He is going to quote himself—

PROUD. I may do—the art of politics is to persuade others to accept you at your own valuation—the art of freedom—

BOAKES. He *is* quoting himself—

PROUD. I am glad you know my humble text so well—is to persistently demolish that evaluation—

GLINT. I saw the book on the remainder stall. As I got off the train. Stack after stack. The price had been slashed. And then the slashing was itself slashed. But did they move?

PROUD. Many a masterpiece is remaindered. Don't be a snob.

GLINT. Ugly little yellow book, complete with Nigel's balding mush and strangulated grin, the man who stood eight times for the leadership—

PROUD. Why do you keep saying eight times, you know damned well I have not stood eight times, there have not been eight—

COIN. Nigel—

PROUD. The day you write a book—

GLINT. I shall write a book. I shall write my memoirs. And they will go to twelve editions—

PROUD. Do you see what I mean?

BOAKES. I think I hate men more every year I come to conference. *(They look at her)* The groin. The power. The grab. The buttock. The whole fetid bullsmell of you lot. *(Pause)* About Raymond. This is what we do. We make him take charge. We resign if he doesn't. We are the shadow cabinet. We insist. We make him wade through blood, old silver locks sticky with gore of dissidents. And at the end his brain will crack, the accusations of disloyalty will kill him. Then we discard him, and our words will all be reconciliation. He will be the executioner, the parish on whom we turn our backs. The party is rebuilt, with one of us as leader. We win the election and rebuild this scarred and scalded land, we water this desert which stinks with rotting decencies and murdered hope. And in the end, Raymond gets understood, he gets understood where he would most want to be understood, in the brains of historians, in dusty seminars he gets his laurels, and we, who are dirtier than Raymond, we take stick. But England's saved. I don't care with what muck attached, no matter how many little twisted businessmen there are and masons whooping it up in clubs, or tarts dancing on tables with their skirts above their arses. We save the place. *(Pause)*.

GLINT. Monica, if there was a leadership election now, I would vote for you. Because I could never say that, and I don't think you could again, either. In all your life. *(Fade)*.

Scene Four

WORKMEN *enter with cables and leads. They are finishing the wiring of the conference hall. Watching them, a lone figure with a stick. The men move swiftly, athletically, in a half-light.*

Rhapsody of the Lighting Unit

TECHNICIANS. Will yer switch it/ I 'ave switched it/ Fuck it, somethin's fused the socket/ Got no power in this circuit/ Over 'ere, Bri, can yer work it?/ What's yer digs like?/ Bleedin' awful/ Give us power!/ No bloody bathroom just a shower/ Where's me stanley?/ I 'ate conference though I'm Labour/ Where's that masking tape I gave yer?/ We 'ad this gorgeous Indian curry/ Give us it or I will 'ave you!/ Up the road there by the statue/ Lovely chicken biriani/ They say cut down expenses/ It's not Indian, Reg, it's Pakistani/ Do you like Betty Grable?/ If yer want I'll book a table/ Women in them days were women/ Anybody been in swimmin'? Spent four hours on the runway/ I am testing, I am testing,/ Second unit down in Saudi/ We were driving in this Audi/ It's Berni's round, I do believe/ *(The lights come on fully)* HOO–RAY! *(Silently, they gather up their tools, as* ISTED, *a Labour peer of 80, speaks)*
ISTED. They came to my cell, three soldiers with staves, or to be exact, pick handles, and they said, you call yourself a pacifist, we will beat you till the blood runs, and if you lift a finger to defend yourself, or put your hands across your face, we will half kill you as a hypocrite. In Shorncliffe barracks, this was. In the custody of His Majesty's Brigade of Guards. And they struck me, jeering at my great size, that such a hugely built man would not protect himself, but submitted to be bled and bruised by men smaller than himself, which was a kind of miracle to them. And then they stopped, one having broken his stave, another having ricked his shoulder, and the third out of nausea, saying it degraded him that I would not resist, and he felt dirty. And they left me on the floor. 1916 this was. In winter. In unheated cells where others had died of hypothermia. And later, as I shivered, the third soldier returned and flung me a blanket, saying I must be Christ, and he wouldn't beat Christ. To which I said that every man was Christ, and he laughed, finding it impossible that Christ was in him, too . . .

(a technician looks at him)

TECHNICIAN. Seen you before, guv'nor.
ISTED. Well, that's very possible.
TECHNICIAN. 'ere, I mean. I did the rig for this last year. You stood there, just like this. Big, but last year you didn't 'ave no stick . . .
ISTED. I am always here on the eve. It is my superstition.
TECHNICIAN. Castin' spells?

ISTED. I expect to see disarmament in my time. And if it cannot be don
    by argument, it will be done by magic. Do you know how old I am?
TECHNICIAN. You're Lord someone, and a codger.
ISTED. I am ninety and Lord Isted. Do you think I will make it? *(The*
    TECHNICIAN *shrugs, moves off. A* WOMAN *is discovered near* ISTED
    You see, if it doesn't happen here, it cannot happen anywhere.
DRUM. What?
ISTED. Anything. This is the convocation of the good. And the less good
    And the hardly good. *(He turns to go)*
DRUM. How did you mean, disarmament by magic?
ISTED. The arguments have all become redundant. The arguments and
    the counter-arguments. Now the life force has begun to assert itself, th
    dark, wet thing that wriggles in the puddle and the blood. It will bear
    down the chorus of the manufacturers and wash away the biscuit
    brains of strategists. Moisture, you see. Women and moisture. Magic.
    (He goes out. DRUM *walks about the hall like a visitor to a Cathedral)*

I Found Myself

DRUM. I couldn't get a ticket for my dad,
    They don't give invitations to relations,
    Old skin baked in the missionary sun
    He won't hear the first public oration
    Of the daughter virgin until thirty-one . . .

    In clean slip and cardigan to match my eyes
    I plan the best impression that I can,
    A plain woman can always walk with poise,
    As for my voice, if I sound like a man
    That's because a teacher has to cope with so much noise . . .

The TECHNICIANS *address her in chorus as they complete their work.*

Seeing Is Believing

CHORUS. We'll write yer speech for yer.
    And even sleep with yer,
    Away from home you'll do it,

    Down them ol' wires it goes,
    Into ten million homes,
    The ME–DI–A!

    And if yer make-up slips,
    Or you get tremblin' lips,
    They'll rid–i–cule yer!

Old men in nursing 'omes,
Admirals like garden gnomes
Will spit u–pon yer,

And chuck things at the screen,
You'll make stockbrokers scream
And police chiefs plan crimes of an ob–scene na–ture!

Lonely geezers in rooms
Will shudder when the zooms
Show your neck na–ked,

No one will listen to
The argument that you
Carefully cre–at–ed

Because they edit yer
Just to discredit yer,
The ME–DI–A!

SIR ROGER CLAXTON, *the eminent political correspondent and broadcaster, rebukes them from another corner of the floor.*

CLAXTON. That is a lie. A redundant lie. A weary, stooping bankrupt lie put about by men of small stature or fevered egotists. It is not believed and it makes my blood boil.

TECHNICIAN. Joke, Roger.

CLAXTON. It is not wise to joke where a man locates his honour. What these people cannot stand is criticism. I love criticism. To criticize is to swallow freedom by great lungfuls. If you think I misrepresent you, reply, and vehemently, by all means. But do not hide behind the weary, stooping, bankrupt lie. *(He has walked towards* DRUM) Don't you love a conference? The spilled guts in the arena, the floor of gore and the shattered limbs of reputation? I have a thirst for it, like some mad mercenary, I must keep going back . . .

DRUM. It's more important than that.

CLAXTON. Is it? I have had four gins. This is a party which suffers and suffers, is crucified and thinks to show its wounds it will only win respect. But the public only say, look, it's being crucified again. Rather as they would laugh at Christ if he was up there not once, but time and time again climbed up to his calvary. Will you have the fifth gin with me?

DRUM. It is a real democracy, that is why it suffers. It's not a racket, or a front, it's a party.

CLAXTON. You are a zealot, are you?

DRUM. It's given me life.

CLAXTON. Did you need life? With your good eyes I am surprised you needed life, I would have expected life to have gone to you.

And a wonderful voice you have. I might have expected to interview you in high office if I had five years left in me.

DRUM. I must go back to my hotel.

CLAXTON. Why?

DRUM. To ring my father.

CLAXTON. I've frightened you with talk of gins. Come back. You are wonderfully authoritative, but not neutered in the least. I find that uncommon in a woman. I am not proposing anything to you, not a thing but comradliness, I mean very simply a chat on the veranda of the Grand. Ring your parent, of course.

DRUM. Thank you.

CLAXTON. And watch the sea with me, I am not a sex maniac, I am Roger Claxton. *(She looks at him)* What about it? I really cannot go on asking, I have my dignity to consider. *(Pause)*

DRUM. Yes. Thank you. *(She goes out. CLAXTON addresses the TECHNICIANS)*

CLAXTON. They say I bully women, do I? *(They work on)* Bully them? I don't, surely? *(The lights begin to rise on the platform)* Well, they like it, don't they? It's when they get indignant—I mean, the intellectual woman indignant is something—is a spectacle so horrid—*(He picks out a workman)* He agrees with me but he won't say so—I mean is a spectacle that makes me—what—unsexed, is it?

Scene Five

As he staggers on, the rising lights show the conference platform with its full complement of LEADERS and OFFICIALS.

CLAXTON. All right, I am drunk, I am—get me a taxi, will you? I am repelled by what I—only minutes previously—had felt the most passionate curiosity about—I don't need a taxi, do I? I'm next door—dark pleats of the skirt go—POOF! *(He fades out, as the TECHNICIANS depart and the scene shifts to the opening of conference)*

DEASY. Ladies and Gentlemen, Comrades—

CLAXTON. Out of the window—straight—out—of the window—

DEASY. Quiet, please—comrades—A am Alan Deasy and it is ma function—ma honour and ma function—in that order—to chair this annual conference of the Labour Party, and to welcome you—A will begin, in ma usual charming way, by issuing a few threats. A am very hard on comrades who speak over time. There is a blue light there. Heed the blue light, please. It is a discourtesy to abuse the freedom of debate, we have a great deal of business, so A ask for—correction, A doo'nt ask for, A demand—your co-operation in getting through the agenda. Doon't arrive late, doon't disrupt the programme, an' yoo will find me a lovable character. Thank yoo. *(He responds to a cry from the floor)* WHO SAYS A'M NOO A LOVABLE CHARACTER? A am, A got bruises to prove it. *(He turns*

to TOYNBEE, *seated beside him)* The speech o' welcome will be made
by the leader o' the party, the Right Honourable—an' for once the title
means somethin'—Raymond Toynbee—Raymond—*(Applause.*
TOYNBEE *stands,* DEASY *sits)*

CHORUS. He sat up late last night,
        To get the tone just right,
        And prove he is no turn–coat,

        His place in history
        Has been a mystery,
        Is he a chapter or a foot–note?

        His mind has corridors
        And filing drawers
        Stuffed full of Eng–lish learn–ing,

        But can he make the speech
        Which will become the peach
        Of his career, or will they spurn him?

ELAINE *(from the floor).* He sat beside me and he said, listen, I am
    ruthless in love. I said, are you asking to make love to me? No, he said,
    I am an Anglo-Saxon socialist. We fuck, we do not make love. This
    was most intoxicating at the time. I remember him smelling of
    mothballs, overlaid on low tide seaweed. He ferreted inside me for a
    while, there was a volley of abuse, and he bit my shoulder. He ended
    up saying he wished he was dead. I explained the loss of virginity is
    frequently an anti-climax. And I left my husband the same
    afternoon.
TOYNBEE. Comrades . . . *(He looks up)* Comrades . . . *(He peers into
    the hall)* We come together at a time when the need for socialism was
    never—and I say this without qualification NEVER—more evident or
    more crying BUT—when this great party—and I say this without
    qualification too it is the greatest party in the history of democracy—
    when this great party is—and we must be honest for God's sake let us
    be honest—least qualified to take advantage of it why—WHY. *(Pause)*
    This is a very grim time. A grim time and ugly. It is the grimmest and
    the ugliest time that any of us can remember and yet we stand—not as
    we should do not—girded for responsibility but—naked and riven with
    contempt why—
TONY *(from the floor).* IT'S YOU.
TOYNBEE. Why has this situation this—dire situation with all its—
    manifold consequences not simply for this party but—for the entire
    nation why—has this criminal degradation taken place it—
TONY. IT'S YOU.
TOYNBEE. Is the business of this conference to close—this chapter
    of humiliation and to write the—book of progress—
TONY. IT'S YOU! IT'S YOU.

TOYNBEE. To convert the reservoir of anger that fills the British
   people into the tidal wave that—
TONY.   IT'S YOU! IT'S YOU! IT'S YOU! IT'S YOU! IT'S YOU!

Song of the Mindless

CHORUS. It's a pain to 'ear 'im speak 'e 'urts my ears,
       All these cliches that 'ave come down through the years,
       As if we could go on the same ol' way,
       What does 'e know of people, can 'e taste their tears?
DEASY *(rising)*. If the comrades doona know what courtesy is I am
   more than happy to show them. There will be a suspension of
   accreditation in the event of any further interuptions of the
   platform. *(Protests)* If you want to protest you can go through
   the proper channels comrade. *(Shouts)* Doon' look at me like
   tha!—all right, do look at me like tha'. It's an improvement from
   where A'm sittin'. Thank you, Raymond, for a speech—
TOYNBEE. I haven't finished.
DEASY. Which will set the tone for a realistic appraisal of . . .
PROUD. He hasn't finished, Alan.
DEASY *(sitting)* Raymond. . . .

Scene Six

GAUKROGER, *by a coffee stall.*

GAUKROGER. Mr Glint, I mean Brian? Perhaps you don't recognize
   me without seaweed in my hair? *(He extends a hand)* Debt eternal.
   Merci. Merci encore. A man who does not 'esitate when the anguish
   of a fellow creature etcetera. Harry Gaukroger. *(He bows.* GLINT
   takes his hand) There is no liquor, so a humble coffee, may I? You
   'ave olympic shoulders to bear an old fool out the water, as if God
   ordained our lives should henceforth be etcetera. Sugar? In some
   indissoluble manner bound. I 'ave the honour to represent Sham
   Hammerton. Light industrial. We 'ave felt the full force of recession.
   I will serve you, you see. May I call you Brian? All I felt was iron
   limbs around me. I love muscle power, and will power, and the man
   at his peak as you are. Will you honour me by listening to an old
   bloke's advice? Then tread it in the carpet like a fag-end, it's this,
   have you a minute? Bide your time. Bide your time.
GLINT. What?
GAUKROGER. I just said it.
GLINT. What—
GAUKROGER *(intimately)*. Bide yer time. Difficult I know. I was
   impulsive, bursting out all over just like you. When I look at you I
   see my former self, I sense the magnetism of the Man Who Will.
       That's you. THE MAN 'HO WILL. And yet you risked the surf for—
GLINT. The water was still—

GAUKROGER. Still to you, a tempest to me—
GLINT. It was a millpond, Harry—
GAUKROGER *(delighted)*. 'e calls me 'arry—
GLINT. That's yer name, isn't it?
GAUKROGER. Bide yer time, the rest are roman candles, all light, no 'eat, am I keepin' yer? Listen, yer got my life in yer pocket, spend it as yer will.
GLINT *(moving away)*. Come to my hotel, I'll buy yer a drink—
GAUKROGER. I won't 'ear of it—
GLINT. All right, don't, then—
GAUKROGER. Buy me a drink? Never think it. Never say it. The drink's on me. I am the provider.
GLINT. Okay.
GAUKROGER. Harry the vintner of Glint!
GLINT. Ciao. (GLINT *goes. Another watches him*).
GAUKROGER. God bless yer prospects, Brian Glint, 'ho will stand England up again! No, I'm not pissed. Brian Glint, 'ho will restore the old fraternity of classes; welfare and opportunity, the miner's boy with one 'and in the till and the other in the duchess's crutch. Socialism à l'Anglais, down with cold men and teetotals! Am I irritatin' you, brother? You 'ave a look of the most almighty peeve.
PARRY. I was on a parliamentary sub-committee with you in 1963. I lost my seat in a boundary change.
GAUKROGER. If I remembered all the geezers I 'ad sat on sub-committees with, brother—
PARRY. You were drunk on fifteen occasions out of seventeen. But not so drunk as to forget to claim expenses.
GAUKROGER. Drunk to you. When a man 'as no spunk in 'im, 'e thinks the world's intoxicated. Come to think of it, I do remember someone with a yellow face. I did not lose my seat, I got central 'eating put in the council blocks. I did not talk about surplus profit, I got the dogshit off the landings. I did not say means of production, I got the porters reinstated, they call me 'arry in the street, not Quintin or Barnaby—
PARRY. My name's Pete and I'm up for selection in your seat—
GAUKROGER. Christ you are, they tell me nothing, the whispering bastards—
PARRY. I don't believe it is the selection committee's brief to inform the sitting member who may be under consideration for—
GAUKROGER. THIRTY SEVEN YEARS I BEEN IN THAT SEAT! Ask the people in the street 'ho—
PARRY. I only mention it out of decency—
GAUKROGER. DECENCY! WHAT! WHAT!
PARRY. You are driving the coffee stall out of business—
GAUKROGER. There goes decency! There goes a man! *(He tries to attract* ISTED's *attention)* Tom Surrey-Bell—I am no disarmer, but Christ, 'e—Tom—THAT IS DECENCY—(*He turns away from*

PARRY) Get away from me before I punch yer—Tom—(ISTED *stops)*
    'arry Gaukroger—
ISTED. I don't think I—
GAUKROGER. They want me out, Tom—dirty little meetings upstairs
    in pubs, the four-eyed plotters—what's yer decency make of that?
ISTED. I think the present state of the party lends opportunities which
    have not existed in my time—
GAUKROGER. No, but 'ave me out!
ISTED. There is certainly a tide of change running—
GAUKROGER *(exasperated).* LOOK, YOU AIN'T THE ONLY
    BUGGER 'HO LOVES PEACE ROUND 'ERE! (ISTED *moves away)*
    Sorry . . . sorry . . . *(He appeals to standers-by)* Thirty-seven years . . .
    thirty seven years . . . !

Scene Seven

In the Leader's Suite.

Gloating Song

ABSOLUTES. There is panic in the suite
        At the Imperial Hotel,
        Raymond's speech was rather flabby
        And did not go down too well;
        They say he has got problems
        With the two halves of his brain,
        He fell asleep in mid-discussion
        And had a nightmare on the train
        In which Brian Glint,
        The loyal lieu—ten—ant
        Struck him with an ice-pick
        Time and time again.
        They cradled him in their arms
        And tried to stop the flood,
        All Labour's culture flowed
        Down the gangway with the blood,
        But there was no Marx and hardly
        Any Engels to be seen,
        Only R.H.Tawney, William Blake
        And J.M.Keynes!

TOYNBEE. What I meant to say . . . and what I did say . . . what I
    thought I said . . . but did not . . . the gap growing between
    intention and execution . . . will you help me, my dear, I do want to
    govern and do it well.
GLINT. It was no fucking good. Was it? It was no effing use at all. I
    say with all respect, obviously. It was tragic with no balls. What did
    ·you think, Malcolm?

ARDSTOCK. Raymond's speeches read brilliantly—

GLINT. No, don't be a prick, I said—

ARDSTOCK. Yes.

GLINT. What?

ARDSTOCK. No balls.

GLINT. What I think is—may I? What I think is—(RUFF *barks*) Are you making that dog bark?

ELAINE. Me?

GLINT. It barks when—

ELAINE. People tell lies. *(Pause)*.

GLINT. Does it? *(He turns back to* TOYNBEE) You will have to speak to 468. You must show your teeth, and red eyeball. They hate you, Raymond, they want to wipe you out the history books. Scatter them, Raymond.

TOYNBEE. Yes.

GLINT. You say yes more like no. Say yes again.

TOYNBEE. Yes.

GLINT. Same. *(He shrugs)*

ELAINE. You are not coming across. I mean, you are coming across, but as milk. I love your milk, but—

TOYNBEE. I present what I have—

ELAINE. Which is beautiful to me—

TOYNBEE. Which is to govern in all fairness and—

ELAINE. I think you ought to listen to me and not shout because I—

TOYNBEE. I am tired of being told I do not come across!

ELAINE. Because I love you and no one else does here. I am your true and actual lover, so listen, will you?

TOYNBEE. Yes. *(Pause)*

ELAINE. You are coming across as milk, and when you shout it is like milk on the boil, it is not blood, you see, I think in a rage you look worse if anything.

TOYNBEE. Well, what am I to do, then? Because I think it is an actual despising of the British people which you are proposing, a despising you are not entirely innocent of—any of you—

ELAINE. I hate them.

TOYNBEE. No, you only—

ELAINE. I hate them for not loving you—

TOYNBEE. That's silly—

ELAINE. They are rubbish. If they were not rubbish they would elect you—

TOYNBEE. They will hear me, they will hear the arguments, they will see the power of the argument and they will—

ELAINE. Oh!

TOYNBEE. Comprehend its relevance.

ELAINE. You know, what is funny about you is that you speak to me— who is your bed companion and wipes your mouth when you are ill— exactly in the way you speak out there—the same language—the same

innocence. You are not a liar. I wish you were a liar, you are done for,
I think, because there is not one bit of liar in you *(She turns to* GLINT*)*
That is why he doesn't come across.

TOYNBEE. You are enjoying this.

ELAINE. In some way I can't fathom, yes.

TOYNBEE. My fall.

ELAINE. Yes.

TOYNBEE. Because if I fall it means the virtuous government cannot
exist. You want to know that. You want to believe good government
is impossible, it confirms your misanthropy, and the misanthropy of
the rabble who have brought us to this pitch. If I fall, there is no hope,
just as if I succeed, it is virtue in office.

ELAINE. You are much vainer than I thought. Much vainer. And that is
why you cannot lie, isn't it? You believe yourself perfect, whereas all
the others, who know they are not perfect, lie in the pretence. Well, I
knew that from your first look. I wanted to marry a saint, to sleep with
a saint. What woman doesn't? *(She looks at* ARDSTOCK, *who stares
at her).*

ARDSTOCK. I couldn't say . . .

ISTED *(entering).* Raymond, my five minutes.

ELAINE. Christ, Tom, you are lobbying into your nineties! Will they
weight your coffin down? You adorable, good thing . . . *(She kisses
him)* Oh, you rare mineral . . .

ARDSTOCK *turns away in discomfort.*

ISTED. We are full of mutual admiration . . .

GLINT. I'm on my way. *(He turns, goes off)*

TOYNBEE. She is soft for idealists.

ELAINE. Don't call him an idealist. They call you idealist. They do it to
rot you. *(To* ISTED) Are you here to save the rubbish heap?

ISTED. If I can't make children, I might save them . . .

ELAINE. If there is Heaven, you are it. Which is why you don't die.
There's nowhere to go. Isn't that right, Malcolm? (ARDSTOCK *grins
foolishly)*

TOYNBEE. I'm sorry, Tom, I'm not speaking to it. *(Pause, of moment)*

ISTED. Why? *(Pause)* This will be the first year you have not spoken
to it. Why? When it's your cause. When you planted it in the
consciousness—

TOYNBEE. I won't.

ELAINE *(shocked).* No, he asked why. Didn't you? *(Pause)* Silence is
also a lie. *(Pause)* Do answer Tom.

TOYNBEE. I think I cannot disarm.

ISTED. It's party policy.

TOYNBEE. It is not beyond debate.

ISTED. Of course not. It will be debated. And it will be policy again.
You can't put your finger in a dam burst, Raymond . . .

TOYNBEE. Nevertheless, I decline to speak.

ISTED. Speak against it, then.

come to me.' My tent. Not your tent. *(Pause)* It is trivial. Whose
hotel we meet in, is, objectively, trivial. But trivialities put end to
end make a steel girder over which he walks. *(Pause, then with decision,
he scrabbles in his pockets)* Never got a piece of paper when you—
(He clicks his fingers to a WAITER) Piece of paper— *(He draws on the
air to indicate his meaning)* No, stupid, piece of—*(Pause)* I must
acquire the art of triviality. Must squeeze my mind down to the size
of Glint's *(The* WAITER *appears with a note pad.* PROUD *writes on
the tray)* No. You come to me. Historic statement. You come to me.
Ranks with the great one-liners of Anglo-Saxon politics. Give this to
Mr Glint. *(The* WAITER *sets off.* PROUD *turns to go. Encounters
BOAKES)*

BOAKES. Where are you going? We've got a meeting—

PROUD *(thrown)* I—

BOAKES. Nigel . . . ?

PROUD. I—*(Then, with sudden decision)* Hey! *(He sees the* WAITER
has gone) Fuck!

BOAKES. What the—

PROUD. He's gone up in the lift, FUCK!

BOAKES. What the hell are you—

PROUD. WHY DON'T YOU SHUT UP, MONICA! *(Pause, he seems to
crumble)*

BOAKES. Do you want a tonic water? *(Pause.* PROUD *holds his head
in his hands. Lightly)* Have you noticed, when we meet it's always in
Brian's hotel? *(She sees* GLINT *cross the floor)* Oh, here he is. Not a
minute early, not a minute late . . .

GLINT *(holding the note aloft)*. Thank you, Nigel, I got your note. A
small and fascinating document. It is extraordinary what small
re resentments people harbour. Even in the great hotel of genius, half
the rooms are full of trivia. *(Pause)* And you came all the same.

BOAKES. Did you speak to Raymond?

GLINT. I said his speech was disappointing.

BOAKES. Yes, but—

GLINT. I said it was time to make his bit of History.

BOAKES. And will he?

GLINT. Yes. He will open the attack on the Left. And you will follow.
Then Nigel, and I will come up last. Cliff face of utter unity.

PROUD. Why you last?

GLINT *(sarcastically)*. Nigel's speaking to me!

PROUD. Why you last?

GLINT. Because I said to Raymond I—

PROUD. Supposing I want to speak last?

GLINT. Supposing you do.

PROUD. No one asks if I—

GLINT. Look, Nigel, if you want to speak last—

PROUD *(pettishly)*. No, no, why draw a line at that? It's really
absolutely arbitrary where the stop comes, why not concede the
whole—

GLINT. It seems to me a rather trivial matter who goes first and who—

PROUD *(madly)*. IS IT THOUGH. IS IT THOUGH. STALIN. *(Pause, calmly)* Look, I do know you. I hope you won't—in an excess of contempt—think I do not know what's going on. I do. And because I lack the energy to fight every inch—every twist in the carpet—does not mean I do not absolutely know—I DO. *(Pause)* All right! (GLINT *looks at* BOAKES). Okay, then. (GAUKROGER *enters*).

GAUKROGER. Oh! Oh! Olympic musculature, in mohair hung!

BOAKES. Who is this?

GAUKROGER. The chandelier catches the red fire of the brow! I have a table laden, eat your way through, I'll pay!

BOAKES. I've seen you before.

GAUKROGER *(bowing)*. Monica, and Nigel, we have brushed shoulders in the lobby!

BOAKES. Ah . . .

GAUKROGER. You too 'ave come to serve the future, there he stands, who plucked me out the water, Harry Gaukroger, Sham Hammerton! The very best wine in this town I 'ave extracted from the grasping inhabitants and stuck it on your table COST IRRESPECTIVE! If they 'ad asked ten times one hundred I'd laugh and fling the money down—my dream, my dream is to be cheated but indifferent, to pay the asking price and jeer at the racketeer's astonishment! Join us, do!

PROUD. This—gift—of eloquence—of Harry Gaukroger's—is something— we have yet to hear exerted in our cause from the back bench—

GAUKROGER. Come again—

PROUD. I said—when did you last speak in the House of Commons?

GAUKROGER. Oh, that place! I hate to interrupt the greater talents, but I boo a lot.

GLINT. He is an old bent bastard and I should have let him sink . . .

GAUKROGER. I am, I am, but if I'd sunk you would 'ave lost my vote, they are after replacing me—look, Hansard is thick enough, ain't it? Some speak, and some vote, some swim and some pay for dinner, come in, all of you, it's on my account.

GLINT. I shall have to satisfy him, shan't I? Or he'll start stealing my shirts. Where's your fan-club, Nigel?

GAUKROGER *(taking her arm)*. Monica, the table waits, we'll stuff and talk of the old days, did you know I was once tipped as a potential minister for power? I was, by Attlee.

(They go off to the dining room, watched by PROUD, *who is isolated for the Chorus)*.

He Could Cry

CHORUS. He could cry,
    He could cry,

PROUD. If it were in my nature I could cry,

I have standards which I won't surrender,
A moral man in politics, how very quaint,
But there are decencies I will not pre-empt,
Everybody knows the spotless man earns only contempt.

CHORUS. He could cry,
He could cry.

PROUD. If it were in my nature I could cry.

To see the party fall into the hands of people
Whose sensibilities are completely blunt,
I feel like Chamberlain must have felt with Hitler,
That a gentleman cannot win against a runt.

CHORUS. He could cry, he could cry . . .

PROUD. It's in my nature but I'm buggered if I'll cry!

During the song, ANNIE *has entered, and stands obscurely at the back.* PROUD *leaves.* BOAKES, GLINT *and* GAUKROGER *stumble out of the dining room.*

GAUKROGER *(supported).* I will tell yer what socialism is, it is the biggest champagne party in the history of the world—that's what it is— you tell 'em that, Brian, and you, Monica—
BOAKES. Yes—
GAUKROGER. Yer cannot love the flesh an' be a Tory—fact! FACT! *(The* WAITER *is staring at this spectacle)* Don't look at me like that, son, as if 'appiness was bad etiquette—*(To* GLINT) If yer can make people laugh yer'll 'ave equality, that's what I tell the comrades 'ho want me out, yer 'ave got fish eyes an' no laughter!
GLINT. Where are you staying, Harry?
GAUKROGER *(To* BOAKES). I will kip under the pier if you'll kip with me—
BOAKES. I think I—
GAUKROGER. Come on, kip with the Glasgow laddies an' talk drivel till the day breaks—
GLINT. Where's your guest house, Harry? Have you got one?
GAUKROGER. I 'ave one, and I am a bad guest to the 'ost, I 'ost the 'ostess, if yer follow me—
GLINT *(To* WAITER). Get him a taxi—
BOAKES. Sweet dreams, Harry—
GAUKROGER *(He staggers away).* Chuck us out, chuck us out—*(He calls back as he trips)* I 'ave rolled down better steps, *(He turns again)* Brian Glint, I like everything you do, you are the general— *(Then, to* BOAKES) Yer see, 'e does not contradict me, no matter 'ow extravagant the praise—it's the sign of greatness— *(To the* WAITER) CHUCK US OUT! Spaniard 'ho thinks laughter is bad

etiquette . . . (*He goes.* BOAKES *turns away*).

BOAKES. I am walking along the front—

GLINT. Good night, Monica . . . (*He turns, as if to go to his room, sees* ANNIE)

ANNIE. I didn't know your room number. So I waited here. Watching you through the Edwardian glass door. And wanting every bit of you.

GLINT. Do you need to stand so—

ANNIE. Do I scare you because I say what I want?

GLINT. In the hall here—

ANNIE. A woman's not supposed to say I want? I do want.

GLINT. I love it, but try the fire-escape—

ANNIE. Your buttock, your lovely tight buttock—

GLINT. Did you say your name was Annie?

ANNIE. Does it matter what my name is? (*Pause.* GLINT *walks a little way, puts his hands in his pockets. They are in his bedroom*)

GLINT. Darling, you try too hard. So hard you make desire feel redundant . . .

ANNIE. It's not redundant . . . Don't you want to fuck?

GLINT. Yes, I want to and I will do, but—

ANNIE. Can you?

GLINT. Don't worry about my side, I shall, don't worry ONLY I CAN'T TOUCH SOMEONE IF I DON'T KNOW THEIR NAME! (*Pause*) Silly. Just a quirk. (*Pause*).

ANNIE. I haven't done this before.

GLINT. What . . .?

ANNIE. Found someone I wanted. Seen him. Wanted him, and found him. Do you know how difficult this is for me? I have gone through my life, day in, day out, and seen men that I wanted, and did nothing. Just wants. Very basic, down-in-the-belly wants, tearing away and making me slightly sick. You go through life like that. I must get free from that.

GLINT. Yup.

ANNIE. So do I have to go through all this lying—being a woman, have to—lay on the string of falsehoods for—violets in the hair for—simple rights? Come together, can't we, in absolute and simple want, swap of pain and pleasure, go away and—I haven't done this before and now I've talked so much it's all gone anyway. How shall I go, down the fire-escape?

GLINT. Can I kiss you?

ANNIE. Because I'm weak?

GLINT. I dunno, I want to kiss you.

ANNIE. Because I'm weak. (*He goes to her*) I hate your politics, incidentally. Or is it incidentally? YOU'RE HURTING ME.

(*He recoils*)

GLINT. I think you'd better go home. Go on, darling, go home.

ANNIE. You see, I—

GLINT. What about me in all this!

ANNIE. You see, I—

GLINT. It's half past one and I—

ANNIE. Trying to make sense of this!

GLINT (*Fiercely*). Shall I tell you what I hate? More than anything I hate the early hour of the morning and a woman talking and a man talking and not saying what they mean and not meaning what they say and cock half up and cunt half wet and NOTHING BUT THE STALE DRY MONOTONE OF DRIVVEL. I AM NOT AN ADOLESCENT POET AND I WON'T. (*Pause*).

ANNIE. Can I get into bed?

He looks at her. She moves. Blackout. Simultaneous roar of an audience. Interval.

Scene Eleven

FENTON, *enters to address a meeting*

CHORUS. He comes in rather late,
　　　　Eyes down and silent gait,
　　　　He's come from six more meet-ings,

　　　　His eyes are red and ill,
　　　　But there is iron will
　　　　Reinforced by your greet-ings,

　　　　He knows this is a war
　　　　Waged across England's smoking floor
　　　　He has the correct the-ory,

　　　　To possess so much truth
　　　　And have to suffer the tooth
　　　　Of calumny should make him wea-ry,

　　　　But you'd die, wouldn't you,
　　　　Just to learn something true
　　　　About this trag-ic nation,

　　　　If logic will not go
　　　　Where he goes don't you know,
　　　　LOGIC'S ONLY STAG-NATION?

FENTON. My nightmare. My nightmare is as follows. It is dawn in
Downing Street. Very early, and vaguely wet. And I find, when I
call for my servant, I am alone in the house. What is more, the
thing that has awoken me is repeated. This is the scream of a low-
flying jet, whose shadow passes menacingly down the street. I put
on my dressing-gown, I go the telephone. But the telephone will
only connect me to the cricket score, which in other circumstances
I might unreservedly enjoy. I experience a certain claminess. I go to
the front door. I draw back the bolt.

CHORUS. Stephen Fenton is insane,
    So runs the press campaign,
    They would even drive him from hell,

    The more he bears their darts,
    The more he wins their hearts,
    Is he Saint Sebastian or Crom–well?

FENTON. The constable is not on the step. I look up to Whitehall.
There is an ominous absence of traffic. I close the door, and bolt it.
I go into the cabinet room. I sit at my desk. I take out my personal
gun. The desk is the same desk used by Gladstone. The gun is a
present from Fidel Castro. I sit, and I wait. Nothing. I wait longer.
I look at the walnut which will soon be soaked in my own blood.

CHORUS. The man who cannot dream
    Will never turn the stream
    And run it through the sta–ble,

    But can you dream so much
    That you get out of touch,
    And find life's turned the ta–ble?

FENTON. I grow tired of waiting. I put down the gun. I pull the
curtains, unbolt the door and walk into the street. The traffic is
back. It is Whitehall as ever was. I stop a man and say, 'I am the
the Prime Minister, do you know me?' Yes, he says, he knows me.
I ask him to accompany me to the House of Commons. He says he
is late for work. I remind him of his democratic responsibilities,
that I am the elected head of government, etcetera, but he is
recalcitrant. I attempt to detain him. He summons a policeman.
The policeman informs me that if I persist he will arrest me for
a breach of the peace, an item of legislation I had long intended to
repeal. I desist, and alone, and improperly dressed, I walk the half
mile to the Commons.

CHORUS. The left will always be
    Obsessed with conspiracy,
    Look how they mutter,

> The River Thames has not been red
> With the blood of the dead,
> But water can change col–our . . .

FENTON. I present myself at the door of the chamber, but find
myself impeded by Black Rod, an institution I had long intended
to dismantle. He expresses in the convoluted language of Tudor
authority the opinion that I may not enter in a dressing-gown. I
attempt to pass him. He attempts to restrain me. I am the fitter,
and relieve him of his rod. I push open the door. The fug of the
bullpen assails my nostrils. I go to my place amid laughter, laughter
occasioned no doubt by my unconventional apparel. But barely
has this subsided when Mr Speaker calls the House to order, and
he calls it in such a way, with such a pale expression, that we cannot
but sense History has laid its hand upon him. A person is coming,
a person, who has, much to her own annoyance, been kept waiting
by my dithering. It is the Queen.

CHORUS. Can you believe in what
> They claim is a plot
> By the rul–ing cla–sses?

> The constitution has small print
> And if it makes you squint,
> Fenton will lend you gla–sses . . .

FENTON. Who enters, and making some brief address, dissolves the
parliament, sending home the elected representatives of the people
and ending the socialist government. It is an appalling dream, but it
serves to remind us, and perhaps that is why I dream it so frequently,
that this country is not yet a democracy, since the sovereignty of
the nation is not settled in you or me or in all of us, or in a majority
of us, but in the person of the monarch whom none of us has
chosen! It will be the first task of a socialist government to remove
all obstacles to the expression of the will of the English, Scottish
and Welsh peoples, because as long as power resides outside the
elected chamber there can and will be endless obstruction to the
execution of our programme!

(Uproar and cheers)

CHORUS. Fen–ton–ism,
> Fen–ton–ism,
> Will make you rock
> And shudder with coll–ision,

> Fen–ton–ism,
> Fen–ton–ism,
> Will not bother with the lock
> It will just bulldoze the pri–son!

Scene Twelve

The beach on a hot afternoon. GAUKROGER, *in despair, and*
LOUISE.

GAUKROGER. I think I might wake up, and there, with 'is wicked
  little smile, will be 'arold Wilson, an' 'e will say, it's all right, I'm
  back . . .
LOUISE *(drily)*. The factories 'ave gone,
GAUKROGER. What's that supposed to mean?
LOUISE. It's gone. What made him possible. *(Pause.* GAUKROGER
  is sniffing)
GAUKROGER. God . . . the little God . . .
LOUISE. 'ang on—'ang on, you're not crying over—'ang 'on—
GAUKROGER. It was Paradise and we never knew it—
LOUISE. Paradise? Are you—
GAUKROGER. IT WAS PARADISE, ASK ANY BUGGER!
LOUISE. It was livin' on lies—
GAUKROGER. What's wrong with lies? I don't mind lies. You don't
  mind lies. Lies are very comforting. Yer can sleep with a lie. Yer
  can dine on one, 'HO WANTS THE TRUTH IF THIS IS IT! *(Pause)*
  I find—do you find this—I 'ave nothin' to say to no one any more.
  Every minute two thousand people die 'ho I could speak to, an' two
  thousand are born 'ho I can't. It's a shrinking constituency. THEY
  WANNA ABOLISH THE SODDIN' MONARCHY! *(He shakes his
  head)*
LOUISE. You *are* down . . .
GAUKROGER. I couldn't go in there again today, I couldn't listen to
  it . . .
LOUISE *(seeing into him)*. So that was why . . .
GAUKROGER. I was unmanned by the crisis of my time. I've never
  failed yer before, yer know that. FENTON 'AS CASTRATED ME!
  Pass us an egg. Never before 'as politics come between me and the
  bedroom, not even in the darkest hour! *(He bites)* Under Wilson,
  what couldn't I do, I don't boast, you know that, but I could
  satisfy two women from midnight to six. People will look back to
  'is day an' say there was some lovin', then, there was some life in
  springs. Not a bad epitaph. CAN YOU IMAGINE FENTON IN A
  BED? *(They see* CLAXTON *wandering over the beach)* Look 'ho
  it is! *(He grins)* SIR ROGER!
LOUISE *(cruelly)*. You perk up for a knight . . .
GAUKROGER. Sir Roger, collectin' shells? *(To* LOUISE) It's Roger
  Claxton—

LOUISE. I know who it is!

GAUKROGER *(on his feet)*. Harry Gaukroger, member for Sham Hammerton. What of the conference, then, your verdict so far, may I pester you?

CLAXTON. It exhibits more forcefully than anything I have witnessed the irrelevance of socialism to the problems of Great Britain—

LOUISE. Bollocks—

GAUKROGER *(to* LOUISE). It's an opinion—

LOUISE. 'E'S A KNIGHT!

GAUKROGER. Come on, don't—

LOUISE. YER DON'T ASK KNIGHTS TO VOTE LABOUR OR THERE'S SOMETHIN' WRONG WITH LABOUR!

GAUKROGER. Brian Glint, though?

CLAXTON. What about Brian Glint?

GAUKROGER. The shadow—

CLAXTON. Thank you, I know perfectly well what his status is, what about him?

GAUKROGER. Do you expect to be seein' 'im much in the studios?

CLAXTON. If I have learned one thing in all my years as a political observer, it is this. That nothing can be ruled out, and no one can be dismissed; that no one is done for, and nothing is disproved; and no ideology, however futile, and no theory, however archaic, or any dogma, however discredited, however deep its patina of blood or suffering, is ever beyond recall. That is what I think. I have a cottage. I am going to that cottage, and I am shutting the door, and I am drinking gin until the gin runs out. *(He goes off)*.

GAUKROGER. Yer'll miss my speech! *(He stops, looks back)* My speech . . .

Fade to black. Rising light on conference in session.

Scene Thirteen

DEASY *opening an afternoon session.*

DEASY. Come on, noo, settle, please, comradès, we were here dead on time, it's you who's late, we have a schedule an' we are keepin' to it, this is item 727 on the agenda, in the yellow book, Nigel has been waitin' very patiently, Nigel—(PROUD *gets up*)

PROUD. The policy of the party with respect to re-stimulation of the economy is based on an injection of three hundred million—three thousand millions I'm sorry, three *thousand* millions of investment capital, raised simultaneously in the money markets and in the form of government subsidies—

ANNIE *enters, and sees* AXT, *who is in the audience.*

I'm Sorry, I Feel Wonderful

ANNIE. Good morning, are we far down on the agenda,
    I had a bath, I washed my hair, and sat down on the beach,
    You look a bit unfriendly, your eyes are tunnels,
    If it helps, I have prepared a little speech . . .

    Will you hear it or shall I give it you in writing,
    Perhaps you cannot stick the sound of my voice,
    I feel wonderful, I wish you'd share it with me,
    Oh, perfect husband, if you love me why don't you rejoice?

PROUD *(persisting)*. To switch investment into those sectors of the
    economy where the greatest and most profitable returns can be
    achieved, and in alliance with the trade unions to—

ABSOLUTES. BOR-ING, BOR-ING—

PROUD. You say it's boring—

ABSOLUTES. Econ–omics, Econ–omics is a trick!
    What do you think the people are, they are not thick!

PROUD. You say it's boring—you don't care how many schools and
    hospitals this country can afford, you imagine that the equipment to
    keep a brain-damaged child alive falls from Heaven, do you,
    because that's what economics is about, that's what planning is
    about—and it's not boring, it's a matter of life or death—

ABSOLUTES. MORE NUCLEAR WEAPONS! MORE NUCLEAR
    WEAPONS!

DEASY. Stewards, please? Where are the stewards? This 'as been
    a rotten year for stewardin'—

PROUD. I am not opposed to heckling, what I am opposed to is
    organized barracking—which is—which is—

ABSOLUTES. Econ–omics, Econ–omics is a trick!
    What do you think the people are, they are not thick!

DEASY *(to STEWARDS)*. Coom on, get in there, and get 'em oot,
    will ye?

AXT *(to ANNIE)*. Who was it?

ANNIE. What's it matter?

AXT. IT MATTERS.

ANNIE. Brian Glint.

PROUD. No, I am not deterred by it, because to be deterred by it
    would be to abdicate a responsibility I have, as the future chancellor
    of this country, to restore to the people of this country their rights
    to a decent standard—

ABSOLUTES *(off)*. BOR-ING, BOR-ING!

PROUD. Yes, it may not appeal to you very much, the wants of
    ordinary people very rarely do—

A Mind Stretched to Bursting

AXT. I thought of bombs when I was younger,
Thought of blowing the statues off their seats,
Tearing bits out of the bellies of the chauffeurs,
The accountants, the butlers and the priests,
It looked certain I would do someone an injury,
But I got over that . . .

I chose to work with the old tool of democracy,
Logic, reason and the power of symmetry,
Not to be angry, not to be all flailing fists,
Berserk with temper and then slashing my wrists,
Was it a defect in my personality,
But I got over that . . .

I have a flaw of violence in me from my dad
Who was forever creeping to a priest,
The sight of him sobbing for a blow he'd
Dealt my mother made me persist
I would rather bleed than raise my fist,
I thought I'd got over that . . .

It's a matter of applying reason to your heart,
Tie it down, examine it, take anger apart,
Blind feeling, spare me blind feeling,
Blind feeling keeps on coming back,
I feel my body has been rescued from the rack,
I can't get over that!

He lifts a chair high above his head, in a paroxysm of pain.

DEASY. There's a comrade holdin' a chair—can the stewards—the four
prongs go to the ground, comrade (STEWARDS *close on* AXT)
ANNIE. It's all right, he's with me . . .

Blackout.

Scene Fourteen

A meeting. AXT, THE ABSOLUTES, PARRY, *others.*

AXT. The rule book, comrades. The rule book. (*Pause*). Now, that's
a dirty thing. I swore at school I would obey no rule, the rule which
cut me whether running or walking because if I ran in one place I
broke a rule and if I walked in another I broke another, you know
what I mean, the great knot of rules on your head and the gag of

rules in your mouth. Subsequently, I wrote, 'The highest dignity of
Man is that he is not constrained but wills his goodness.' I wrote
that at 21, a free youth; free to possess nothing, free to sleep under
bridges, free to starve and free to love no women. I was heavy on
dignity, you understand, but a little light on life. And then I saw,
the rule gives freedom—it gives freedom to him who makes the rule
his own. A rule is given or received, and I had received it, and now I
wanted to give it. The rule book, comrades The rule book.
(*Pause*) Now, that's a lovely thing! We take it, and we re-write it, not
forgetting when we grow fat with complacency, the rule book will
be stolen by the lean . . . The rule change we require demands the
power to recall MPs. (*He introduces* PARRY) Peter (AXT *sits*,
PARRY *stands*)

PARRY. Good. Good. This is a very good meeting. I think the size of
this meeting is an indication of the passion which the subject of
rule-changing does arouse. Good. Good to see so many. (*Pause*) My
feeling—(*He stops*) My feeling? My conviction! Is that this
resolution must be supported. Why? Because the onward
movement of socialism calls for transformation at all levels of a
machine which has not yet been seen to serve its purpose—the
spreading of power, not the the centre, but to the periphery, the
transplanting of democracy outwards from Westminster and not
inwards from—New stuff from you.

RONY. New stuff from you.

PARRY. Not new.

RONY. Not said all this—

PARRY. Have said it—

RONY. Not on record. Not in 'ansard when you 'ad a seat.

PARRY. That was a different age.

RONY. It was an' all. (*She grins*) New from you, but lovely.

TONY. We are all bussin' to the future. DING! DING!

PARRY. We will pass this resolution on Thursday, and if we do not pass
it, we will bring it back next year, and if it does not pass next year, we
will bring it back again, and again, and—(*As he sits,* GAUKROGER
appears)

GAUKROGER. I am on my way to dinner, so I shan't keep yer—

ALISON. Invitation only—

GAUKROGER. So I shan't keep yer—

ANNIE. Got an invitation, 'arry?

GAUKROGER. I am, I think, the member for the constituency which
'as backed this silly bloody resolution—

SUSAN. No swearing—

GAUKROGER. Three things—

SUSAN. We don't have swearing—

GAUKROGER. One. You 'aven't got a chance in bloody 'ell—

SUSAN (*shooting up*). Can we have a resolution making swearing in a
public meeting an offence?

GAUKROGER. Two—
SUSAN. Please, Mr Chairperson?
GAUKROGER. Two—you 'aven't got a chance in bloody 'ell—
AXT. We will take a no-swearing—
GAUKROGER. And three—you 'aven't got a chance in bloody 'ell!
MALC. Shove off an' get yer dinner—
GAUKROGER. What d'yer think? Yer gonna 'ave a parliamentary
   Labour party parrotting your instructions in the 'ouse?
AXT. It's called democracy.
GAUKROGER. Democracy? Wha'd you know about democracy? I was
   on a coal cart—
MALC/SUSAN. THE COAL CART! THE COAL CART!
GAUKROGER. I was! I was on a coal cart, an' a baker's van an' a milk
   cart carryin' democracy to people 'alf of 'hom were dead before you
   got shot out of yer mother's bum!
RONY. Mother's BUM?
GAUKROGER. That's my service to democracy! 'ave you ever spoken
   to a worker in your life?
RONY. Mother's BUM?
AXT. That is corrupt and irrelevant—
GAUKROGER. I said 'ave you spoken to a worker in yer life?
AXT. We do not descend to that—
GAUKROGER. No, yer wouldn't would yer—
AXT. GROVELLING AND SORDID CLASS DISHONESTY—
GAUKROGER. Grovellin' and" sordid 'e calls it—
AXT (*taut to breaking*). MANIPULATIVE HYPOCRISY—
GAUKROGER (*looking at him*). You're shudderin' . . . you're
   shudderin' . . . you should see a doctor, son . . . not go tryin' to
   take my seat. . . . (*Pause. RONY goes up to AXT, who is stiff with
   suppressed fury. GAUKROGER starts to leave*) You could never
   'old it . . . none of yer . . .

Blackout.

Scene Fifteen

The Conference Hall. The platform, entire but for GLINT.

DEASY. 4-6-8 . . . . . 4-6-8 . . . .
PARRY (*from the stand*). A register? A register? Is this a party or the
   stock market? Register what? A faith? A passion? How do you
   register a passion, Raymond? How do you measure an ideal? Put it
   in the scales, do you? It sounds like a job for the Department of Trade.
   Get the inspectors in. (*Laughter*) I will remind Raymond, in case he
   hadn't noticed that this is not the Department of Trade, it is the
   Department of Belief! (*Laughter*) It is the Department of Hope!

(*Cheers*) It is the measureless idealism of the English, and the Scottish and the Welsh peoples, and it will not be chopped or trimmed! There is only one measure of a man's faith, and that is his determination! (*Cheers*)

DEASY. 4-6-8 . . . . . 4-6-8 . . . .

PROUD. Where is Brian?

BOAKES. Have you rung him?

PROUD. All I get is the answering machine.

BOAKES. Well, ring the police.

PROUD. Ring the police?

CHORUS. Where is Glint, Where is Glint,
    The platform's under pressure,
    Where is Glint?

APPS (*on the stand*). They tell us, we must be proscribed, though proscription hurts, that we must be registered, though registration is abhorrent, that we must be expelled, though expulsion is repulsive! They wince, they weep, you could almost pity them, couldn't you, really, you have to extend sympathy to men and women obliged to carry out such unwholesome tasks!

TOYNBEE. I know this speech . . . .

APPS. I have a message for these unfortunate and tear-stained creatures—please, don't suffer on our behalf—end the registration, end the proscription, end the dictatorship of the party bosses and the union bosses who are one great sobbing chorus of dismay! Please, no more tears of pity, you will break our hearts! Don't cry as you stab democracy in her eyes! If you can't be honest, at least be consistent, and laugh like a butcher should! (*Massive applause*)

TOYNBEE. That is my speech. I made it in 1954.

CHORUS. Where is Glint, Where is Glint,
    The platform's under pressure,
    Where is Glint?

PROUD. I will find Brian, and I will knock him across the floor.

BOAKES. From behind.

PROUD. From any fucking angle . . . .

DEASY. Card vote card vote, tellers please.

CHORUS. Where is Glint, Where is Glint,
    The platform's under pressure,
    Where is Glint?

Freeze on conference. Naked, BRIAN GLINT *is standing in his bedroom.*

GLINT. Oh, my silence . . . . Do you hear my silence? (*Pause*) The Man Who Would Not. (*Pause*) Split the Party. (*He turns to* ANNIE) The power of NOT. The Honour of NOT. The great, eloquent, unforgettable NOT. (*The platform again*)

DEASY. Card vote . . . . Card vote . . . . tellers, please! (*Hands go up,*

bearing massive numbers. DEASY *descends to the* TELLERS, *who
go among the* DELEGATES) 37 . . . . 48 . . . . 27 . . . . 61 61
. . . . 51 . . . . 8 . . . . quiet, please 40 . . . . four–0 . . . . 99 . . . .

GLINT. Raymond will win, and it'll be the finish of Raymond. He will
be tainted, and I'll be clean. As he falls, I'll rise, the lift going up,
and the lift going down . . .

ANNIE. Celebrate it. (*He looks at her*)

GLINT. Say I own you.

ANNIE. Nobody owns me.

GLINT. I do, I own your feelings, so I own you.

ANNIE. That turns me on but it's rubbish.

DEASY (*Attempts to declare the result against a racket*). The voting is
as follows—the voting is—well, do ye wanna hear it or doon' ye?
(*Racket*) Oh, coom on, it's noo a bloody football match—no, friend
it's noo a football match, ye took the wrong bus—(*He leans
theatrically on the table, one hand on his hip. Pause*) I am noo makin'
a declaration until—(*It continues. He sits down. There is a disturbance
at the front. He leaps up*) IF YOU COOM UP HERE A WILL PUNCH
YOU ON THE NOSE BROTHER, A'M TELLIN' YOO—

TOYNBEE. I will make the declaration—

FENTON. I'm sorry, Raymond, you cannot make the declaration, it is
out of order—

TOYNBEE (*ignoring this, to* DEASY). I will make the—

DEASY (*to his opponent*). Okay, then, A'll coom doon there—(*He starts
to leave the platform*)

TOYNBEE. Do not leave the platform! Alan!

BOAKES (*standing*). Comrades, there are twenty million people watching this!

FENTON (*to* DEASY). Just read out the vote.

DEASY (*turning on him*). It's your bloody mob down there

FENTON. That is not a democratic sentiment, Alan, and you know it—

DEASY. I said this is your bloody mob—

FENTON. You mustn't be frightened of people. This is a socialist party.
It's about people—

DEASY. Ooh, ye fuckin' pious bastard— (FENTON *shrugs,
graphically*. DEASY *turns to the microphone*) DO YE WANNA
HEAR THE VOTE OR DOON' YE? (*Calm sets in*) Resolution 468,
requirin' the registration of groups within the party, for the
resolution—Six million, four hundred thousand, eight hundred an'
eighty-eight—(*Boos and uproar*) Against the resolution—two
million, six hundred thousan'—(*He is drowned out.* TOYNBEE
stands, transfixed by power)

CHORUS. Now we must celebrate
        Democracy is safe,
        It's Raymond's fin-est hour,
        Look what scheming leads to,

It hands you over to
A weak man who loves pow–er!

His Bride Rises

AXT. I have lived with anger all my life,
      It slept beside me, woke beside me, my true wife
      Whose love stayed bitter every hour of the night
      Gave me no peace but clamoured for her right,
      How I could envy all the satisfactory men,
      The murderers, wife batterers or clerks
      Who by every stroke of knife or pen
      Approve the world, endorse its crimes,
      Kiss the shark's fin . . . .

DRUM. It won't last

AXT. You know that do you?

DRUM. Been here before, haven't we? 1950, 1931–

AXT. Oh, you good woman, laying your faith to be trod on, and your
      spirit to be whopped into dough . . . .

DRUM. Don't be superior.

AXT. They are tearing up my card . . . .

DRUM. Yes.

AXT. For six years I was impotent. I could not make love without the
      world getting in at the window, crying pain and degradation, on my
      naked back all the goblins . . . See the goblins? Say hello! (*He stoops,
      quickly*) And now I am out. Goblins again.

DRUM. Don't be rotted by Toynbee. Toynbee will go, like a corpse
      into a mattress, into the horsehair, into the springs . . . .

AXT. And then it's Glint.

DRUM. Fractionally better.

AXT (*bitterly*). Fractionally. When there is mass murder. Fractionally,
      she says . . . .

DRUM. Yes. (*She turns to go*)

AXT. My wife fucks with Glint. (*She stops*)

DRUM. Why are you telling me?

AXT. Because you–(*He closes his eyes*) Because I am sick, and dog
      tired with the strain of being me, and could pour it all out to the
      first good ear that listened, my bones are breaking, little cracks
      inside my head, the strains, the splits, the hairline fractures, why
      are you so calm and green-eyed, rather ordinary and obviously a
      perfect woman? For the first time I understand how people can
      live on mountain sides in huts waiting for the death that comes, like
      plague to the feudal crofter, over the hill, that old renunciation,
      that old God . . . .

DRUM. I voted for your resolution. On Socialist relationships. I'm
      sorry that it failed . . .

AXT. Don't go . . . .

Scene Sixteen

The stand. ISTED *waits, weighing silence.*

ISTED. You've got no right to be alive (*Long pause*) Nor has this
building any right to stand. Nor the cathedrals. Nor the tower blocks.
Nor the beech trees down the rich man's avenue. No right. (*Pause*)
By any application of the most unstrict logic, you should be dead,
and not just dead, but fine dust. You are here by the most fantastic,
circumstantial, coincidental tricks of fate in the history of the world,
HOW LONG DO YOU THINK IT CAN LAST? (*Pause*) It is not a
way to live. It's a nightmare. It is a hideous infliction worse than
any plague or ravage and it takes away your freedom. What is your
freedom worth, the freedom that this party and this people have
struggled to attain over five centuries? You are less free than any
helot of the ancient world, or feudal serf, who if he died, at least
knew his children did not, or if his children died, at least knew his
neighbour did not, or if his neighbour did, at least the village over
the hill might not—you have no such confidence! You have only
the blank and hideous certainty that when this happens, AND IT
MUST, your family, and your race, and your culture, and your genes,
your entire impression on this spinning rock WILL BE ERASED.
(*Pause*) Don't run away with the idea you will not be erased. No
hope of it. It is erasure. Universal. And all the medicines, and all the
kidney machines, and all the literature, and all the love and all the
passions are RUBBISH against this fact of your erasure. The slave, no
matter how flayed, might run, might take his chance. The tortured
man might see a child pass his prison cell, and know, after his
torturing, times change. But you know nothing except extinction.
THERE HAS NEVER BEEN A SLAVERY LIKE IT. It mocks this
democracy! It laughs in the face of your so-called choice! It hangs
over you, and not over you alone, but over what you carry in your
blood, and in your semen, and in your womb. What your parents
gave you, and what links you to your ancestors, and what you hand
on, your place in that endless chain which is the greatest comfort of
mortality, THEY ROB YOU OF THAT! (*Pause*) Try to think about
it, even though it drives you mad. It is better you are mad, and can
neither sleep nor eat, than that the human thing should perish. We
must disarm now. Every minute is a gift, now. Is a piece of luck.
Every second an unearned gem. We must disarm NOW. (*Pause*)
Move to the doors quietly, and disarm, NOW. Do this before some
false step sets the rockets off. Remember, you have no right to be here
any more.

*He stands, swaying slightly. There is a great silence, then an uproar of
cheering.* ELAINE *goes to the stand, kisses his hand. Blackout.*

Scene Seventeen

The beach. ARDSTOCK *stands in the shadows.* RUFF *barks.* TOYNBEE *appears, exercising his pet.*

TOYNBEE. Who's there? (RUFF *barks*) Come on, who's there?
ARDSTOCK. Me.
TOYNBEE (*suprised*). What are you . . . . in this . . . .
ARDSTOCK (*with a shrug*). Looking for love . . . . (TOYNBEE *stares at him*) You know . . . the chip smell in the hair of vagrant youth . . . the groin beneath the arches . . . you know, Raymond, lose my flaming wick . . . .
TOYNBEE. Are you drunk?
ARDSTOCK. No. Lord Isted is a communist queer, I have the evidence.
TOYNBEE. What?
ARDSTOCK. You 'eard.
TOYNBEE. What?
ARDSTOCK. A Major in the KGB. I have the evidence.
TOYNBEE. You have the—
ARDSTOCK. Oh, come on, stop your bloody daft blinking in the flashlight—
TOYNBEE. Why tell me in this—
ARDSTOCK. Dogshit sea-front, well why not? (*Pause*)
TOYNBEE. You're mad.
ARDSTOCK. Oh, if only I was. I myself would rather be straight-jacketed than tell you—
TOYNBEE. Tom Surrey-Bell a—
ARDSTOCK. Unbelievable! A red aristocrat! A poof in the KGB! I've never 'eard of it before, either—
TOYNBEE. Look, Malcom—
ARDSTOCK. I tell you, obviously, before I have to make this known. Prepare you so we can—
TOYNBEE. This is the last thing I—
ARDSTOCK. Make the necessary statement in parliament. (*Pause. He looks along the alleyway*) Look, the way they stand there, isn't it—brazen? You cannot touch 'em, not with love or anger . . . the very degeneracy of love . . . . (*He starts to wander off.* RUFF *barks wildly, snaps at* TOYNBEE)
TOYNBEE. Ruff—Come here—and—Ruff— (*sound of low growling*) Show me your teeth, would you, what—CHRIST! (*He grabs his heel. The dog bounds off*) Come here! Heel! Heel! You've never been out in a town before, you—HEEL! (*The dog disappears*) I am the master! I am the master!

He goes out. Daylight on the beach.

ANNIE (*strolling*). Last day, and the little deals go crack like seaweed in the sun. The manifesto is written, and the delegates go—

AXT. The delegates go—crack—

ANNIE. You see, I've come back and nothing's—

AXT. Pop go the delegates . . .

ANNIE. Not stained, not altered, just the same old—

AXT. Dry men, and dry women, like twigs—

ANNIE. What is it?

AXT. It must be moist. It must be passionate.

ANNIE. What? (*Pause. He looks at her*)

AXT. Socialism.

ANNIE. Must be—

AXT. I CAN'T GO ON WITH IT (*Pause*)

ANNIE. I've driven you a little bit mad. I've gone out and spent three nights with someone. And you've gone a bit mad.

AXT. I met a woman. And she's stained me. And altered me. And I haven't touched her yet. And may not. (*Pause*)

ANNIE. Oh, 'eck . . .

AXT. And all this—can't save us because it isn't passionate—

ANNIE. Oh, Christ, he's gone and—

AXT. 'ELP US!

ANNIE. WHAT ARE YOU ON ABOUT YOU SILLY—Look, I 'ave a saying. If it can't go into a resolution, it's not worth saying. Take it to the branch, John.

AXT. I shan't lie with you again.

ANNIE (*blankly*). Shan't—(*She rounds on him*) WE'VE GOT A KIDDIE PLAYIN' AT 'IS GRANDMA'S!

AXT. I shan't lie with you again.

ANNIE. Lie with? What's this lie with? You'll be callin' spunk seed in a minute, and fuck a union

AXT. IT IS A UNION (*Pause*) Don't smash it, please. This feeling I 'ave. Don't bash it up with sarcasm.

ANNIE. It's not sensible.

AXT. It comes that way because—

ANNIE. It's not rational—

AXT. Like poetry because—

ANNIE. It's codswallop in the bluebells—

AXT. DON'T HURT MY FEELINGS WITH YOUR BRAIN. (*He looks at her. She goes off.*)

GAUKROGER (*entering*). I 'ave waited forty years for this. Brian says to me, it's down to you now. You inaugurate my campaign for the leadership. The theme is unity.

LOUISE. I'll frame it in the hallway.

GAUKROGER. 'arry, 'e says, when you go up, to cough will be a crime, to shift a foot, a scandal. Pins will sound like falling scaffold. The dust will be audible, like snow . . . . 'ow do I look?

LOUISE. A man. I could pass you in the street, and think a little unclean thought . . . .

GAUKROGER. Come 'ere—

LOUISE. Frank's in the vicinity—

GAUKROGER. No, no, come 'ere— (*Suddenly he buries his face in her shoulder*) 'ave I been good to yer? 'ave I given yer pleasure?

LOUISE (*puzzled*). 'ere, what's this—

GAUKROGER. There 'ave been better lovers, but'ave I—

LOUISE. Don't talk like you're gonna die, you're only makin' a speech—

GAUKROGER. Yer gave me the greatest, greatest, pleasure—

LOUISE. Oh, 'ell, you daft—(*She embraces him. FRANK wanders in*)

FRANK. My socialism is a pilgrimage. I was over there, by the dustbins, and I thought, it is a pilgrimage ... (*He stands, as GAUKROGER detaches himself from LOUISE*)

GAUKROGER. Wish me luck, Frank ...

FRANK (*stuck to his theme*). A body of people ... walking in fellowship ...

GAUKROGER. Back for dinner.

LOUISE. Be good. Be thunderin'.

GAUKROGER (*waving*). I launch Brian Glint, like a pebble from a catapult ....

CHORUS. He walks along the street,
    On slow, reluctant feet,
    Drawn by the public houses

    If only he was late,
    He would miss the debate,
    Or fall and tear his trousers ..

GAUKROGER (*stops, takes a swig from a hip flask*). If I stand on the platform, 'ho is gonna say THAT IS THE MOMENT THE WORLD CHANGED? Nobody. My appearance is a speck of dust which falls upon the scales but does not tip 'em. (*Pause*) Yer could argue. (*He walks, stops again*). Who do I serve by appearing? No one. Ain't there enough words in circulation without you addin' yours? Rather, by my silence, I display THE DIGNITY OF LABOUR MAN. (*Pause*) Yer could argue ... (*Pause, then, unpersuaded, he moves on. Then he stops, takes out a coin*) 'eads I go, tails I don't. (*He spins it*) Fuck, it's 'eads ... (*The dog RUFF appears, whining*) 'ello, 'ello, 'ho's this? down, then, down a bit ... (*It nuzzles him, licks his face*) Yer lost, are yer? Got no master? There ... there ... Expensive too, by the look of·yer coiffure ... (*He looks round quickly*) Can't abandon an 'elpless animal, can I? Well, can I? No this 'as buggered me speech, this 'as ... buggered it ... (*It whines encouragingly*) Get down ... get down on yer 'aunches an' I'll give yer me speech ... (*The dog sits, appreciatively*)

He never Called It a Faith

GAUKROGER. Comrade, I speak to you not from the 'ead but from
the 'eart,
I 'ave no truck with intellectuals, politics ain't science, nor is it an
art,
It's only puttin' dinner onto plates
An' buyin' drinks for workmen and their mates—
Comrade, I speak to you not from the 'ead but from the 'eart,
Be realistic and don't upset the apple cart,
I 'ave been in this world for sixty years so take my 'int,
We can't 'ave 'arold Wilson so let's 'ave Brian Glint,
Comrade, I like my life so please don't take it apart,
I speak to you not from the 'ead, but from the 'eart . . .

AXT (*returning, hearing this*). Oh, Labour . . .
GAUKROGER (*getting up from the floor*). Why ain't you in the
Conference?
AXT. I'm out.
GAUKROGER (*smugly*). Miss yer on the GMC. (*Pause*) Forgive us.
I am a vindictive old shit, but I never liked yer. Yer thin, and
'aunted, an' when I look at yer I see England burnin'. . . .
AXT. It is burning. It's burning now.
GAUKROGER. Paranoid. (*He shrugs*) Good word, that. Paranoia.
Never 'eard it a few years ago. I was gonna get that in somewhere . . .
'the mindless paranoia . . . . . ' you know . . . (*suddenly,*
GAUKROGER *starts to cry*)
AXT (*bewildered*). What—what—
GAUKROGER (*through sobs*). I was 'oping . . . when I left . . . when
I kicked it . . . I would . . . leave things as I found 'em . . . but . . .
they're breakin' everything up . . . FORGIVE US.
AXT. Come on, get . . . (*He supports him*)
GAUKROGER. FRANK! WHERE'S FRANK?
AXT. Frank who?
GAUKROGER. WHAT'S SOCIALISM, FRANK? WHAT IS IT? I've
forgotten what it . . . FORGIVE US, FRANK . . .

Scene Nineteen

DRUM *is seen in the conference hall. She stares up at the deserted
platform. Pause.*

DRUM. I got my resolution through. By a two-thirds majority, which
according to the constitution of the party, ensures it becomes
official policy, is written into the manifesto and will become
legislation under the next Socialist government. I attended forty-
seven branch meetings, fifty meetings of the executive committee,
and eleven meetings of the General Management Committee. (*Pause*)
One hundred-and-sixty hours of my life.

Pause. The CHORUS *takes up 'The Curse of Debate'. Fade to black.*

* * *

Downchild

CHARACTERS

TOM DOWNCHILD	A journalist
STOAT	A delinquent youth
OLD BEVIN	A farm labourer
YOUNG BEVIN	Another farm labourer
LADY HEYDAY	A political secretary
ROY SCADDING	A former Prime Minister
MOSCROP	A vicar
LANA	Wife to Young Bevin
MOLLY	Mother of Heyday

ACT ONE

Scene One

A field at the cliff's edge. A man is standing waist-high in the wheat.

DOWNCHILD. Wonder, would I like to be a wedded queer? Ringed the
matrimonial dick? Half an unheroic couplet? What is it Wystan says?
The rinsing of souls in marriage? Spotless little intellectual fucks?
Poet up poet? **Where are you, criminal?** Recollections of the great
Greek buggers. Foreskins couchant on Aegean rocks. Behind
taverna shutters the bray of public schoolboy and the public schoolboy giggle. **Come on, I'm bursting!** I wouldn't swop their mouldy
communion for one toss in a Liverpool urinal. **Not for one asphalter's
grunt!** Oh, there you are . . . (*He stares into the sky*) Aren't the
birds bright? On the down draught, beaks half-open in—(*Pause*) Oh . . .
You are . . . You really are . . . For a thug, luscious . . . For a savage,
quite divine . . . . (*He slowly disappears into the wheat. Two*
LABOURERS *appears, carrying scythes. They throw them down. One
proceeds to roll a cigarette*)
OLD BEVIN. 'Eard 'un lass night, did 'ee? Screamin' an' what bother
not, eh?
YOUNG BEVIN. 'Eard 'un? Seen 'un! 'As 'anging off wisteria stark
bollocker as ar cum back from Beggars. In motor 'eadlamps.
Proper shit me, don't mind tell 'ee, pop.
OLD BEVIN. T'is 'im as killed un peacocks, likely.
YOUNG BEVIN. Likely.
OLD BEVIN. Bites 'em, don't 'e? 'eads arf?
YOUNG BEVIN. Seen 'un?
OLD BEVIN. Not seen 'un. Not seen nothin', thank 'ee, Christ.
YOUNG BEVIN. Shit on big 'ouse.
OLD BEGIN. Ditto.
YOUNG BEVIN. Sez I as shouldna. Sez I as keeps my chevvy tickin'
on 'un. Shit on big 'ouse all the same. (*He reaches into his bag for
a flask.* DOWNCHILD *emerges from the wheat*)
DOWNCHILD. Good morning! (*The* LABOURERS *look at one another*)
You till a lovely soil. I can smell Devon from twenty miles off.
The passionate air! (*He extends a hand*) Tom Downchild, novelist,
poet, beauty addict, priest of wit and slave to scandal. I had my ear
to the ground, was listening to the sea burst in the caves below, then
heard your lovely accents, up I stood. (*They still appear bewildered*)

Come on, you've seen strangers before, I shan't blight the crops.
(*A youth,* STOAT, *stands up in the wheat some yards away. The*
LABOURERS *look at him*) My great grandfather was a shepherd.
On the Cheviots. He drank cold tea.

YOUNG BEVIN. S'nart cold tea.

DOWNCHILD. Not cold tea? What is it, then? It's from my ancestors
I get my love of fields. The hay fever's a problem, but I am of the
opinion you can cure any illness with a view. I am the author of a
book called *Scenic Therapy.* In it I prove all cancers can be cured by
a simultaneous glimpse of an ice-field and the high sierra. Unfortunately the means to effect this combination has yet to be discovered.
(*The* LABOURERS *look at one another, pick up their things*) Oh,
don't go! Don't go! I so enjoy a conversation! (*They start moving
off*) Who's the lunatic? (*They stop*) Come on, I cracked your
dialect. (*He reaches for his wallet, holds out a five pound note*)
The agricultural wage is a screaming scandal. (*Pause, then* OLD
BEVIN *reaches for the money*)

YOUNG BEVIN. Shud na, pop.

OLD BEVIN (*stops*). Why not, thun?

YOUNG BEVIN. Shud na, thass all.

OLD BEVIN. Shit on big 'ouse, says thysel'.

YOUNG BEVIN. Maybe.

DOWNCHILD. Whose is the house?

OLD BEVIN. Sum tart.

YOUNG BEVIN. Pop.

OLD BEVIN. Sum tart, I says.

YOUNG BEVIN. Don't tell 'un nothin', pop, am warnin' thee!

OLD BEVIN. Tell 'un nothin', get paid nothin', don't us, stupid? Use
'ead to get thy dinner, says I. (STOAT *bobs down in the wheat again*)

YOUNG BEVIN. Strangers is piss in beer, old 'un, I tell thee.

OLD BEVIN. Bollocks. Buy tha' fifty throws of one-arm bandit, for
coupla words.

YOUNG BEVIN. S'no matter, shut thy gob.

DOWNCHILD. My wrist is weary from keeping aloft this five pound
note. Would you be quicker if I made it ten?

OLD BEVIN. Wha'?

DOWNCHILD. Doubled it. But don't tell me what I can discover
flicking through a phone book. (*He looks down quickly*) Hello,
someone's bored . . . .

YOUNG BEVIN. Shove on, pop.

DOWNCHILD. Not now, naughty . . .

YOUNG BEVIN. Shove on, I tell thee!

DOWNCHILD. Barry . . . inopportune . . . inopportune . . . .

OLD BEVIN (*snatching the notes*). Lady Heyday!

YOUNG BEVIN. What did I tell thee? Shut gob, I said! Geroff, ol'
bugger! Shift thy bloody arse! (OLD BEVIN *hurries off*)

DOWNCHILD. Lady Heyday? Ten pounds for that?

YOUNG BEVIN (*going off*). S'na in fuckin' phone book, tell 'ee tha'!

An' don't do fuckin' in our fields, as lose yer dick cum harvest, bent
bugger. (DOWNCHILD *watches the* LABOURERS *disappear. Pause*)

DOWNCHILD. Barry . . . . call it a day, eh? (*Pause. He still stares after
them*) **Come on!** (STOAT *stands up again*) Appetite gone dead on
me. Sorry. Urge fled before a stronger power. (*He looks at* STOAT)
The chariots of passion scattered by the bows of curiosity.

STOAT. Wha'?

DOWNCHILD. Never mind.

STOAT. **You keep on sayin' never mind! I do mind!** (*Pause.*
DOWNCHILD *looks at him*)

DOWNCHILD. Catullus.

STOAT. All right.

DOWNCHILD (*gazing about him*). What lovely countryside! What
gorgeous dells and streams, hot fields shimmering, and madmen
clinging to mossy walls. I adore the country! Steam and fever, bare
buttocks in the hunter's dung!

STOAT. Wanna drink, Tom.

DOWNCHILD. I come to tread on flowers, thread pimpernels in the
delinquent's hirsute crack. But no! Down goes my foot, through
puffballs, mildews, splitting barks alive with rot! Am I not a
charmed man, Stoat? Am I not the absolute in journalists? The
ground opens wherever I walk, spews up its secrets. And they
accuse me of invention, call my column—what, the libel factory?
Never! Their sin flies to me like filings to a magnet.

STOAT. Tom. Pub.

DOWNCHILD. I should have found her, yokel or no yokel. Takes
more than a sea-breeze to blow away the odour!

STOAT. **My fucking drink.**

DOWNCHILD. Stoat! My precious Stoat! I am ignoring him in my
excitement! I see a little malice in his eye—there—just a tiny yellow
glint, a shade that creeps across the iris in the lull before the blow,
last light glimpsed by startled victim . . . old woman edging by the
post office . . . poet with shoulder bag . . . the arthritic . . . the
artistic . . . twitching on the kerb . . . .

STOAT. Not criminal.

DOWNCHILD. Beg pardon?

STOAT. **Not criminal.**

DOWNCHILD. Not criminal? Not criminal! Would you be here if you
weren't criminal? Would I look twice at you if you weren't criminal?
Don't hide your light! I wouldn't piss your shoes if you weren't
criminal. I wouldn't point your dick with tweezers. Kiss me.
(STOAT *stares*) Kiss me. Criminal. (*Pause.* STOAT *kisses him*) I
missed you. I thought of all the lovely sins of Wandsworth, the
little acts I wasn't party to. Night after night—no, be honest with
my love—one night at least, I wandered underneath its walls, past
screws no doubt accustomed to the parallel patrols of the bereaved,
and stared hard at the bricks as if to tell you that my cock was big.
Which it was. Under my Burberry. So big. Always that bigger by

myself. Why is that? Longing to ask them, was he happy? Was he being laid? By whom? A right froth of interest your scraped bonze must have created, nudged by murderers and extortionists. What chance did I have, a dying sapling in his memory?

STOAT. Thought of yer.

DOWNCHILD. Often and often?

STOAT. No. Now and then.

DOWNCHILD. You flatter me. I was sick with jealousy.

STOAT. They 'ad no words, just grunts. They were twice in prison, first in Wandsworth, then in their vocabulary. A very tight cell. They could 'ardly move. I met a banker on the landing. Taught me loquacious and tenacious. Two things 'e never was.

DOWNCHILD. Say if the scenery's too much for you. I thought it would revive you after the monotones of gaol. but it might make you dizzy, like a diver brought up fast, give you the rural bends . . .

STOAT. Never bin to Devon.

DOWNCHILD. Picked it with a pin. The day before you got remission. That hayfield, I said— I had the two-and-a-half inch to the mile—that hayfield is where I shall pluck Stoat again. Stoat willing I will drink him to the sound of larks.

STOAT. Was willing.

DOWNCHILD. Was. Four hours from Wandsworth's baby door. I drove like a pissed divorcee to a cowboy's bed. Smell that? It's sea.

STOAT (*stripping off his shirt*). White! Am I white!

DOWNCHILD. I like you white. But sunbathe if you must. Look like any road driller.

STOAT. Ta, I will. You fetch the beer. (*He lies down, out of sight in the wheat.* DOWNCHILD *starts to go, stops*)

DOWNCHILD. I wasn't faithful to you. Obviously. (*Pause. There is no reply. He goes off. After some moments, a* WOMAN *enters, elegant, poised. She stops*)

HEYDAY. The sea. Look. (*A* MAN *appears behind her, slightly stooping, with a stick*)

SCADDING. Seen it.

HEYDAY. Tray of gold.

SCADDING. If you say so.

HEYDAY. Beaten brass. Blazing. Molten something.

SCADDING. Ann, but for my back I'd say down in the wheat, love, torn stockings, beetles in our pants . . .

HEYDAY (*ignoring him*). Gulls say agony, say agony . . . !

SCADDING. Do they?

HEYDAY. Agony of freedom!

SCADDING. Really? Can't speak gull language myself. (*Pause*)

HEYDAY. You mustn't be wilfully philistine. You really mustn't. It belittles you. Chops feet off your stature.

SCADDING. She cares about my stature.

HEYDAY. Yes.

SCADDING. You're too kind.

HEYDAY. Silly.

SCADDING. I'm sorry, Ann, but looking at you, find it very hard to think of gulls, what gulls want, speculative philosophy of gulls, etcetera, think only there stands a woman I once had naked over desks, once scattered all the efforts of the civil service with our shifting rumps, spilling into papers, juicing over their reports. That is the tenor of my thoughts, I must admit. Not gulls. Forgive me. I should think gulls, obviously. (*He pretends to stare at the sky*)

HEYDAY. I am tired of my attraction. Do you understand that?

SCADDING. No.

HEYDAY. Tired of wanting to be wanted. Say you understand that.

SCADDING. No, I don't.

HEYDAY. Enjoying my deadness. My coldness. Loving it. (*Pause*)

SCADDING. Pity. (*Pause*) Pity when all the way down here I thought— you imagine—she will do this to me, she will do that to me—does she still wear that bra I like—will she shave her armpits—will she leave a little hair—I'll kiss her in this place—I'll kiss her there—she'll sit astride me for my back pain—what will she taste of—and her breath—always ate apples when we met—sweet for one another—kill the cigarettes—I chewed through a Granny Smith outside your driveway—

HEYDAY. Oh, no . . .

SCADDING. Oh, yes—our old habits—lay my head on her brown belly —catch the little odour of her juice—her rough-soled feet will up and down against my shin—her nicotine-stained fingers scarcely touching —but just touching my—pity, pity, what are the gulls saying? Can't quite catch it. Agony, is it?

HEYDAY. Bitter.

SCADDING. Well, I am of course. I am a philistine, after all.

HEYDAY. Come back to the house, now. (*She starts to move away*)

SCADDING. Tell me one thing. This one thing, absolutely truthful, please. Being out of office, is it, has done this? Without the leadership, I look a seedy thing? (*Pause*) My resignation cost me dear, then? (*Pause*) Christ, what do you fuck?

HEYDAY. I don't know.

SCADDING (*She looks at him*) I would have gone on governing. I would! I would have staggered through if I'd known this!

HEYDAY. Silly.

SCADDING. Silly, yes, but would have.

HEYDAY. Is my cunt so very wonderful? (*Pause*) Is it? (*Pause*) Such a very special thing? (*Pause*) You make me feel bad. It would be so easy just to let you—

SCADDING. Yes.

HEYDAY. Out of pity? Would you want that?

SCADDING. Yes. (*Pause*)

HEYDAY. No. Never do anything for pity. Pity's dead. (*She kisses his cheek, goes off. SCADDING stares out to sea. There is a sneeze from the depth of the wheat*)

SCADDING. Oh, you bastard. (*Pause*) Up, you bastard. (*Pause*)
Got to get you, have I? Fetch the crawler out the crops? Whip in!
Whip in! (*He surges into the wheat waving his stick*)

STOAT. Ow! You fucker!

SCADDING. Am I! Am I, though?

STOAT. My scalp, you cunt!

SCADDING. Struck one! Caught one nasty! Lay on, foxy! Sneaker!
You bastard earhole in the wheat!

STOAT (*writhing under blows*). Leggo, will yer?

SCADDING. Can have no peace, eh? Can't dawdle with a woman, can't
I? Can I piss unspied on, please, you cack-collecting poop thief?
Where can I be, in Christ's name snatch a minute, eh? Have mercy!

STOAT. Ow!

SCADDING. Have mercy, eh? (DOWNCHILD *appears, holding two
bottles. He watches this spectacle*)

STOAT. My bleedin' brain!

SCADDING. Have mercy, then!

STOAT. **All right! All right!** (SCADDING *stops beating him*) Don't
'ave ter knock me eyes out, you ol' cunt . . .

SCADDING. Think the ground's against me, sometimes. Tread on
pebbles and they squeak . . . (*He goes out*)

STOAT (*hands to his head*). Disloged me meninges, the bugger . . .

DOWNCHILD (*staring after* SCADDING). Oh, you have been
honoured . . . .

STOAT (*shaking his head now*). Is it dark?

DOWNCHILD. Honoured, I repeat . . . .

STOAT. **'As it gone dark!**

DOWNCHILD. To take stick from the mighty.

STOAT. Bruised me irises . . . **'alf blind, fuck it!**

DOWNCHILD. Well, this is a stumble, such as the very cock of newsmen get in their lifetimes only once. How did you meet him?

STOAT (*grabbing a bottle*). Give us that.

DOWNCHILD (*as* STOAT *pours beer over his head*). Stoat? How did
you meet?

STOAT. Never met 'im. Come an' clobbered me. **Is that blood?**

DOWNCHILD. What did he say?

STOAT. My poor bloody 'ead . . .

DOWNCHILD. Stoat, I cannot tell you how the condition of your
scalp pales into insignificance when I am so agog to discover how
you came by it.

STOAT. What a sentence, Tom—

DOWNCHILD. Out with it!

STOAT. **I got concussion.**

DOWNCHILD. Quick, then, before it floats out of your memory. (*Pause.*
STOAT *prepares*)

STOAT. I was lying in the grass there, letting the kind ol' sun soak into
me leather, thinking 'ow in Wan'sworth sun was god, we marked 'is

passage inch by inch across the landing—

DOWNCHILD. Substance now, eh? Trimmings later.

STOAT. When I'm bothered, bothered by a geezer and a tart—

DOWNCHILD. Tart?

STOAT. Blonde, I thought, goin' by 'er accent—

DOWNCHILD. Which was—

STOAT. Unnatural. Out a bottle.

DOWNCHILD. Posh, though?

STOAT. Posh, but out a bottle.

DOWNCHILD. Heyday.

STOAT. Wha'?

DOWNCHILD. Go on.

STOAT. 'o prattle filth.

DOWNCHILD. Filth?

STOAT. 'e says can I 'ave you—she says not—why not, 'e says—

DOWNCHILD. Too quick.

STOAT. You know, the usual! An' then 'e charges in an' clobbers me. I sneeze, see. Fuckin' grass.

DOWNCHILD. Be more specific.

STOAT. **My 'ead 'urts.**

DOWNCHILD. Stoat, I promise you your bruises will have satisfaction. Now tell it to me word for word.

STOAT. No! (*He soaks a handkerchief in beer, mops his forehead*) Just a dirty conversation. (*Pause.* DOWNCHILD *looks out to sea*)

DOWNCHILD. You see, Stoat, there are conversations and conversations. I have leaned against the porcelain in any number of piss palaces and heard better sonnets from stinking cubicles than got in fussy volumes, tart statements and epigrams rolled off the tongues of tramps and queens to make my book-learned earholes gape with wonder and my imagination shrink with shame. To no end, though. Their treasures will run down the tiles like spit or spunk. But should Virginia Woolf say Happy Christmas when it's Easter, this becomes the cream of wit, gets carved in History. What you just overheard, Stoat, was an historical flirtation. Banal it may have been, basic to the edge of stale. But not one of his thousand speeches, nor all his brilliant Hansard patter, will lodge in the public mind like this. We will have him celebrated by posterity, down for all time as the man who said 'I'm coming, get your knickers off.' Or what. Do you follow me, Stoat? That was Roy Scadding scraped your bonze. (*Pause.* STOAT *is staggered*)

STOAT. Scadding? 'im?

DOWNCHILD. Almighty God as was. Who dragged us into the new age. Who made stupor rhyme with socialism and selfishness a passion. Him of the dirty cuffs and fingernails.

STOAT. It was. **It fuckin' was.** (*Pause*)

DOWNCHILD. I adore your bewilderment. Could kiss your poor, downtrodden daze. But give it to me word for word now, while it's fresh. And include the tensions, where he bullied her, where he used his eloquence to get her stripped. Quick. (STOAT *is rocking to and fro*) Stoat? Stoat? (*Pause.* STOAT *is weeping bitterly*) Oh, are you angry, little, tiny, criminal? Do you feel dirtier than ever, now? (*He kneels beside him, kisses and caresses him. Lights fade to black*)

Scene Two

Night. A figure is standing in the wheat.

DICKER. Oh. Um. Ah. By the way. **What!** (*He laughs, shudderingly, stops*) Er. (*He clears his throat noisily*) Listen. **Who said that!** (*He giggles uncontrollably, stops*) **No, you can't! You can't, so there! Because I said so! Yes, I did. I did, so there, shut up, shut up, shut up, shut up!** (*Pause. He takes deep breaths*) I have wandered and I apologize, but I did want to see the sea. Not from a car. Not even with the window down **I'm sorry I am not in uniform!** But actually see it, with my own eyes, and sniff it, on my own, my very lovely own nose on my own. **The uniform's behind the door! I know it is!** I do so little on my own. **Not true!** Not true. Not true. All right, not strictly true, not true in **can I get a word in, please!** Am always on my own, I grant you, by the most strict definition in my own company, yes, practically all the time, I meant however I **meant.** (*Pause*) I meant, thank you, I meant under my own **direction. Of my own free will. What!** Thank you, thank you, thank you. **I have a little boy, you see.** (*Pause*) Well, it is a lovely night, it is, it really is, I love it, do you, love the moon on water, seascapes, oh, I do, I do, flowers, hills and trees, I go all, go all **shuddup you cow** go all **shuddup, shuddup,** go all **shuddup!** (*Pause. He looks quite calmly out to sea.* HEYDAY *appears, hands in the pockets of her cardigan. She looks at him*)

HEYDAY. Chilly lick off the sea tonight . . . . (*Pause*)

DICKER. Sorry.

HEYDAY. Yes, but are you? (*Pause*)

DICKER. No.

HEYDAY. I do want to have this out with you. To stress upon you how very strongly I do feel. How vital it is you co-operate.

DICKER. Yes.

HEYDAY. How absolutely, wholly and utterly impossible this is.

DICKER. Yes.

HEYDAY. To threaten, if you like.

DICKER. Quite.

HEYDAY. Because we have to be entirely certain this won't—what with peacocks—become the talk of Devon, don't we?

DICKER. Yes. (*Pause*)

HEYDAY. How do I know, then?

DICKER. What?

HEYDAY. You'll be good? (*He shrugs*) Got the whole run of the garden.

Not a small plot, either. Not a pocket handkerchief.

DICKER. Know every blade of grass. By name.

HEYDAY. Maybe.

DICKER. Know what time the daisies go to bed.

HEYDAY. Yes.

DICKER. Now! Want to be up someone now!

HEYDAY. First thing tomorrow.

DICKER. No! Now, now! (SCADDING *appears, leaning on his stick*)

SCADDING. Oi. Too loud. (*Pause.* SCADDING *jerks his head,
    indicating* DICKER *should leave.* DICKER *walks off stiffly.*
    SCADDING *looks at* HEYDAY. *Pause*) What makes these buggers
    scream all night? (*He looks up at the sky*) Love, is it? (*He goes off,*
    HEYDAY *looks towards the sea, then turns to go*)

DOWNCHILD. Good evening! (*She stops, turns to see* DOWNCHILD,
    elegant in overcoat) I left my colleague deep in an encyclopaedia,
    reaping knowledge, any knowledge beginning with a C. Capitals, he
    was on to. Did you know Guatemala was the capital of Guatemala?
    I didn't. God knows how many brain cells exhaust themselves
    sustaining that useless piece of information in my head. I like a
    walk at bedtime. The 40-watt bulb in the lampshade hardly serves
    to silhouette the corpses of dead flies. Are you local? Will there be
    a storm? (*She looks at him, taking him in. Pause*)

HEYDAY. No. (*She turns to go*)

DOWNCHILD. I haven't enjoyed a cliff so much since Galway. Very
    similar, except in scale. And Galway cliffs are granite. More vertical
    and barren. They pitch less, too.

HEYDAY. Then where's the similarity? (*Pause*)

DOWNCHILD. The mood. I'm an artist, you see. Moods are my
    speciality.

HEYDAY. I must be going.

DOWNCHILD. Oh, don't say so! There is a moon tonight to set lovers
    at one another's buttons and madmen crashing at their bars. They
    will be dispensing tranquillizers by the gallon at the institutions. Much
    overtime will be worked in the wards. Some bruising. Some
    dislocation, I predict. Look at it shining on the sea! You could walk
    on it!

HEYDAY. Good night.

DOWNCHILD. There is no institution round here, is there, Lady Heyday?

HEYDAY (*stopping*). Who?

DOWNCHILD. You heard me, I think.

HEYDAY. You've made a mistake.

DOWNCHILD. Me? Never! I'm a card index of celebrity!

HEYDAY. Really.

DOWNCHILD. As noses go, you have one of the finest. I'm not fond
    of the things myself, but you can't pick a face to pieces, can you?
    It's all knobs and indentations. A fraction more of knob and people
    turn away, a fraction less and everybody wants to kiss you. I'd
    know your profile in a hood. (*Pause*)

HEYDAY. There are no institutions.

DOWNCHILD. Ah. (*Pause*)

HEYDAY. Who are you?

DOWNCHILD. I thought you'd never ask. Kevin McMin, Novel Laureate of All Ireland, foremost exponent of the Epic Gaelic style, sole creator of The Shimmering Banner, all eight volumes, bled from my heart and eye.

HEYDAY. I'm afraid I'm not acquainted with your work.

DOWNCHILD. Why should you be? It's not in print yet. As soon as the situation permits, funds for publication will be set aside. In green leather, the Movement has stated, with silk marker, orange. I was crowned at sunset in Ballina, on the allotments, naked to the waist, the vine leaves tickling my hair. At five pistol shots the tricolour was flung across my shoulders. Somewhat economic, given the austerity of war. (*Pause*) Alias Tom Downchild. Alias Lord Cocky of the Daily World. (*She stares at him. A terrible pause*) Somebody died once when I mentioned that. Buckled, grew small, and died. I tried to breathe into his mouth, but there was so much vomit coming out of it I naturally recoiled. (*Pause*) For that I had my fingers broken by a bunch of squires. (*Pause*)

HEYDAY. Leave me alone.

DOWNCHILD. You won't believe this, but—

HEYDAY. Leave me alone.

DOWNCHILD. Purely to entertain my friend, him of the encyclopaedia, in search of views—

HEYDAY. **Do, for Christ's sake, do.** (*Pause*)

DOWNCHILD. I was saying, what brought me to this luscious place was only holiday. Silly, giggling holiday And lo, I come across at midnight, between Guatemala and the Horlicks, the face that blocked a thousand bills and towered topless in Westminster . . . . . . History, that, though, isn't it?

HEYDAY. You are here to persecute me.

DOWNCHILD. Really! I have only to walk in a room and people call for cheque books, dogs or bouncers. Can't a man relax?

HEYDAY. How long are you staying here?

DOWNCHILD. Well, that depends.

HEYDAY. On what?

DOWNCHILD. My friend. I think I can say as long as it takes to get a tan. He will have his tattoos on a honey background.

HEYDAY. You are a liar, obviously.

DOWNCHILD. Obviously. (*She stares at him for some moments*)

HEYDAY. I do not understand—I do not honestly understand—how you can do a thing—can spend a life—dedicate intelligence—spill precious time—in so ravenously—consuming—shit. In sniffing laundry. In lying under beds and licking stains. When you are no fool. When the world is so very hungry for business to be done. What is it? I do not understand. (*Pause*)

DOWNCHILD. It's a funny thing . . .

HEYDAY. Give me a little peace now. I am chewed, digested, defaecated, dried and scattered by the winds. Give me some peace now. (*She starts to go*)

DOWNCHILD. The food is swill where we are staying. The Beggar's Arms has got three shit-pans in the Bad Food Guide. Why don't you invite us to dinner? (*She looks at him, goes off. He watches her disappear*) Oh, Tom, Tom, Tom! She is such a **dishonest slag!** Her crisp white blouse! So clean-handed, poised, frail-fingered, twisting the stems of dried flowers, tugging at her pearl-string in the emptiness of her spinsterish days! How could you, Tom, what are you, Tom, it could be **your own mother, Tom!** (*There is a terrible cry off.* DOWNCHILD *freezes. The moon disappears behind a cloud. The cry reverberates, fades again)* Moon. (*Pause*) Moon? (*Pause*) **Come on, moon!** (*He pulls up his coat collar and turns to stride away. He stops dead as a figure bursts out of the wheat behind him, uniformed and hideously gas-masked*)

ST LEGER. **Eng-land and St Le-ger, Ho!**

DOWNCHILD *shrinks inside his coat, not daring to turn. The figure plunges away. Pause. The cry is heard some way off.*

DOWNCHILD. Stop shuddering you pathetic old queen.

The moon comes out. Pause. Then DOWNCHILD *strides off. Instantly, Bach organ.*

Scene Three

Interior of the parish church. An organ playing. STOAT *enters warily, overwhelmed by the sound;*

STOAT. **Shuddup!** (*The music stops.* A CLERGYMAN *appears. Pause*)
MOSCROP. Why?
STOAT. 'urts me. Rollin' down the cavities inside my 'ead.
MOSCROP. Beauty hurts you.
STOAT. Kills me. (*Pause.* MOSCROP *looks at him, turns to go*) What's a tym–typ–
MOSCROP. Tympa–
STOAT. **Don't 'elp me!** (*Pause.* STOAT *gathers his resources*) Tym–pan–um. (*He smiles*)
MOSCROP. Silly old word.
STOAT. **No it's not!** (*Pause*) No words are stupid. No words. (*Pause*) Thank you for giving me a word. (*Pause, then* MOSCROP *starts to go again*) **What is it.** (MOSCROP *stops*) Is it a winder?
MOSCROP. No, it's not a window, it's a–
STOAT. It is a door?
MOSCROP. Warm.
SOTAT. Warm, am I? (*He walks a little, gazes around*)

MOSCROP. Warmer. (*He stops*)

STOAT. Clue. (MOSCROP *looks at him*) Give us a clue!

MOSCROP. High.

STOAT (*looking up, then turning to* MOSCROP *with a grin*). It is a semi-circle of masonry above the lintel of a door. In this instance the setting of a fifteenth century wall paintin'. (*Pause*) S'in the guide. I signed the book. Not signed it. Made my mark. My stoat. My slim quick mover.

MOSCROP. We are honoured.

STOAT. You are, my ol' sarcastic. I wrote, I scratched, 'An Evil Atmosphere.' Mis-spelt, of course. I did not write 'Lovely little church' or 'Near to God'.

MOSCROP. No.

STOAT. Not me.

MOSCROP. People are so ugly. And so dull.

STOAT. I passed an ol' bag by the graves, 'o whipered, fluttered at my passin', like I was black dog or the devil, shook she did, like I'd found 'er out, some 'ound 'o'd sniffed her tracks from London.

MOSCROP. Mrs Heyday.

STOAT. 'Ow would I know? And I was torn, torn in two, whether to nut 'er to the ground, so as to satisfy 'er expectation, or pass by, like a warning.

MOSCROP. Terrible dilemma.

STOAT. It was, my ol' sarcastic, it was. In the event, I passed by like a warning. (*He looks hard at* MOSCROP, *wanders a little*) The more words I get, the less inclined I am to nut. A peculiar thing. And as if to recompense me, 'ardly am I in the door, I pick up—tympanum. Christ knows when I shall find a context for it, but words are like dicks and muscles, perish from lack of use—(*He stares up*) What a fine tympanum! I 'ad one over my cell door. 'ad cunt from Playboy in it. (*With a glance at* MOSCROP) Well, you gotta look natural. (*They both stare at the painting*)

MOSCROP. Saint Sebastian.

STOAT. Lovely figure, slender. Could never love a fat saint.

MOSCROP. They come from Yokohama, Kansas, Düsseldorf, whispering banalities in every tongue. Last year one tried to pass under the lych-gate in a Buick. Our dumb peasants' war memorial, this is. Down came the slates for this yank's pleasure.

STOAT. You suffer.

MOSCROP. Yes.

STOAT. From nerves and hate.

MOSCROP. Do I.

STOAT. Oh, you do, you do. I see it in yer eyeballs, swivellin' a bit. So much venom, so little elbow. I come across it time and time again in H.M. Prisons. This could be a prison, the door inside the door, coats of arms and stuff. Oh, blimey, look 'o's 'ere . . . . (DOWNCHILD *walks up the aisle*)

DOWNCHILD. There he is.

STOAT. Peace, Tom.

DOWNCHILD. Peace, he says.

STOAT. God's 'ouse?

DOWNCHILD. God's house, he says. (*He stares at* STOAT, *sits in a pew*) I'm silent today. Take my meaning from my looks.
(STOAT *rubs his nose uncomfortably, shifts, begins a conversation*)

STOAT. You were sayin'—what was it—about beams?

MOSCROP. Beams?

STOAT. Yeah, you know, beams. Old, was it?

MOSCROP. Old, yes.

STOAT. And, er—go on—

DOWNCHILD. The deliquent English boy. His fatuous endeavour to communicate.

STOAT. I thought you was silent today!

DOWNCHILD. When he is not a menace, what is he? Pitifully squirming, foot to foot . . . .

STOAT. **Shuddup.**

DOWNCHILD. Inside his skull a vomit cocktail of ignorance and useless facts, long words floating on a sea of unfathomable passions, bottomless oceans of ancestral dark. Study his eyes, and you can see Celts running, hear men with hairy faces barking at the moon. I am silent today, incidentally.

STOAT. I wanted to be by myself.

DOWNCHILD (*looking at* MOSCROP). I notice. And I was by myself, involuntarily. Nude bathing solo. Jacksie in the breakers. Thank you for the memory.

STOAT. I 'ave to be alone sometimes!

DOWNCHILD. Oh, the sound of him! His precious soul! I weigh upon it, do I? Suffocate? (*He looks to* MOSCROP) Don't mind us. This is routine bickering, the squirming of a fine mind in fetters, futile protest of a comic slavery.

MOSCROP. This is a place of worship.

DOWNCHILD. And I am worshipping. Much against my will. I'm knee bent to the Prince of Darkness here.

STOAT. You always 'ave to degrade me! Ain't I low enough you 'ave to degrade me? All right, I am degraded! 'appy, are yer?

DOWNCHILD. I do hate it when he fights back. Such powerful words. He wounds me!

STOAT. Whatcha want me to do? Prostrate myself? I will! All right? I will! (*He lies down on the flagstones*) Prostrated, right? Lick, lick, lovely dust, delicious, tasty beetles!

DOWNCHILD. Get up, you embarrass me. Prefer your spiteful little kicks.

STOAT. Fore'ead on the venerable pavement, right? Knock, knock! All because I missed the beach, all because I—

DOWNCHILD. No! (*He gets up, walks a little way*) Because there are not many beautiful moments in this life. Because they are so few you have to treasure them, and hoard them, and lick and love them,

that's why, because I was hewing out a memory, that's why. (*Pause*)
Us, the dawn, the surf, etcetera. Wet skin, fine sand, salt lips, etcetera.
I could have thrived on that for years, took it out and polished it,
sitting at my desk in stinking Fleet Street, in the rattle of dead
conversation and the yelps of typists, could have sucked it till my
mind was sweet. But no, he wants to be alone . . . .

STOAT. Do it tomorrer . . .

DOWNCHILD. **Do it tomorrow!** What do you think these moments
are? Currency? You can't mint them! (*He throws himself into a
pew*) God forgive a man his wasted appetites. And there are poets
walking about with brainless girls . . .

STOAT. Might not 'ave worked . . . . (*Pluckily*) No two lovers are ever
thinking the same thing at the same moment . . .

DOWNCHILD. He quotes me.

MOSCROP. It is a fact. It is an ugly, chilling fact.

DOWNCHILD. It's a fact you can do nothing with. I hate that sort of
fact. Give me a fact that I can work on. Like this. What is it screams
at night round here? (MOSCROP *looks at him warily*) Apart from
beaten wives and sheep in labour? (*Pause*) Come on, vicar, don't
tell me the vicarage has triple glazing. (*Pause*) What? (MOSCROP
looks evenly at him)

MOSCROP. You have heard St Leger.

DOWNCHILD. The place is full of saints.

MOSCROP. It's a surname. He has yet to be beatified. St Leger, VC,
whose name is foremost on the lych-gate. Colonel of the
Devonshire Dragoons. He fell in Macedonia.

STOAT. Fell?

DOWNCHILD. Government for killed, Stoat. You can always trust a
poet to lend authority a word. When?

MOSCROP. 1918. In a futile battle. In a God-forsaken place.

DOWNCHILD. It shouts a lot of filth, but I suppose even a saint might
in its final moments. They're only human, after all.

MOSCROP. He led a hopeless charge against entrenched positions. The
soldiers were his workmen, carters, foresters, ploughmen off these
fields. Their names are on the lych-gate, too. For the first time in
their lives they faltered in their loyalty, dropped their rifles, turned
and fled. But not St Leger, shouting over bombs and bullets,
'England and St Leger, Ho!' The family motto.

DOWNCHILD. Heard it.

MOSCROP. All this according to the sole survivor, shot through the
cheeks but spared by the opposing peasants. They fell back,
leaving their raving officer exposed. Then came a whizz-bang which
clanged off his head, severed it neatly so it rolled and bounced down
the rocky Balkan slope, gathering momentum, rolled quicker than the
soldiers fled, overtook them even, ghastly object which shouted
terrible abuse at them, rolling its eyes and shaking blood, 'cowardly
buggers!' cried the blueish lips, then bounced down a ravine to
become an eagle's lunch. Posthumously, they decorated him, a

squire betrayed. And he had given them Christmas dinner at the manor house. His wife stopped that. (*Pause*)

DOWNCHILD. You tell it like a poet. What happened next?

MOSCROP. Nothing, for sixty years. Then the arthritic survivor, who never slept without the echo of machine guns in his ears, encountered his CO in the woods on its first appearance. He fled, for the second time, and died soon after. They say his wounds bled.

DOWNCHILD. From shame, no doubt. And did it have a head, the apparition?

MOSCROP. Yes.

DOWNCHILD. Odd. I can't think why it waited sixty years to manifest.

MOSCROP. It was completing its aborted life span. All St Legers die at ninety.

DOWNCHILD. And where are the St Legers now?

MOSCROP. Sold out. One is in Bermudan real estate. Another lives in Guernsey. (*Pause*. DOWNCHILD *gets up*)

DOWNCHILD. When I was privileged to hear it, the poor creature reiterated with all the tedium of a mania, its wife was being shagged by dagoes. Whatever that means. Slang, is it? Mentioned hotels on the riviera.

MOSCROP. It does, I believe.

DOWNCHILD. Peculiar.

MOSCROP. Yes. Are you staying very long?

DOWNCHILD. Everybody asks me that. Yes. No. Who are you?

MOSCROP. Moscrop, the Right Reverend. (*Pause*, DOWNCHILD *goes towards the door, stops*)

DOWNCHILD. I'm a poet myself. Can you think of a rhyme for sphincter?

MOSCROP. There is no rhyme for spincter. It's arhymal. (DOWNCHILD *begins to go*. STOAT *follows*. DOWNCHILD *stops*)

DOWNCHILD. Oh, don't feel you need to follow me. Don't feel any obligation to be my spaniel. A mind as complex and as rich as yours must be alone at times, to freshen and regenerate .... (*He looks from* STOAT *to* MOSCROP, *goes out. Pause*, STOAT *looks bitterly after him*)

STOAT. I will kill 'im one day. I will kill 'im.

He goes out. MOSCROP *doesn't move. After a few moments,* SCADDING *appears. Pause.*

SCADDING. My God. My God is all understanding. Knows me. Knows why. Comprehends necessity. Makes allowances. Do you know my God, John?

MOSCROP. Yes ...

SCADDING. I have come to lay myself before Him. To say to Him, you know the crevices of my mind, and every little itch therein. I have to do a murder. What does He say, John? (*Pause*)

MOSCROP. He says, is there no better way?

SCADDING. Tell Him no.

MOSCROP. He isn't happy.

SCADDING. No more am I. Help me to—

MOSCROP. Door's not shut. (*He goes, returns*)

SCADDING. Help me. Help me kneel. (MOSCROP *assists*
SCADDING *into a kneeling position*) Oh, this cold stone . . .
Jesus, it shakes me to think of all who've knelt here, English
knights and virgins. Makes me shameful. Makes me small. My
life! Ask Him, have I done wrong with it?

MOSCROP. No, He says.

SCADDING. Oh, generous God! You see, He pities me!

MOSCROP. Profoundly.

SCADDING. Not done yet, though.

MOSCROP. Go on.

SCADDING. With murkiness.

MOSCROP. Go on, He says.

SCADDING. If He lends me His pity, I can do it. Otherwise not.

MOSCROP. I'll intercede.

SCADDING. Then it's mayhem. I'm not thinking of myself.

MOSCROP. He knows that.

SCADDING. You know who I'm thinking of.

MOSCROP. Yes.

SCADDING. Her. And England, too.

MOSCROP. He knows this.

SCADDING. Christ, He is merciful! I wouldn't be! I wouldn't be!
(*Pause*) We have to send old Lucky to Him. To His bosom, quick.

MOSCROP. What?

SCADDING. Ask Him.

MOSCROP. **What!**

SCADDING. Shut up and ask Him for a sign. Strike me dead if He's
against it. Ask Him. (*Pause. MOSCROP'S eyes are tight shut with
effort*)

MOSCROP. He disapproves.

SCADDING. What!

MOSCROP. He disapproves but—

SCADDING. What—

MOSCROP. Knows nothing is absolute—

SCADDING. That's right—

MOSCROP. Knows sin from sin—the sin pure and the sin relative—

SCADDING. Good, good—

MOSCROP. The sin vile and the sin necessary—

SCADDING. He understands! He understands! This is a God! Will
He strike me dead, then?

MOSCROP. Wait. (*Pause*) No.

SCADDING. Thank Him. Thank Him. (*He leans forward and kisses
the ground. He stays thus for a long time*) Can't get up.
(MOSCROP *is staring into space*) John. (*Pause*) Can't get up.
(MOSCROP *helps him to his feet*) I've done nothing in my life

without a prayer.

MOSCROP. Murder . . . .

SCADDING. Lucky's gone bananas, John. You know it. Beyond bananas, if that's possible. He was bananas to begin with. And the St Leger ghost is wearing thin.

MOSCROP. Yes.

SCADDING. Nine times out of ten he goes out in civvies. One night some gang of ghost-hunters is going to catch you in a net.

MOSCROP. Quite.

SCADDING. We have no option, do we, then? (*Pause*) Don't have to answer that. (*He turns to leave*) Tell Ann, will you? She balks at it.

MOSCROP. Extraordinary function for a priest . . .

SCADDING. She listens to you. She thinks you have something, something not to do with brains. Ann thinks she's anybody's equal, which is why she argues so. But in spiritual matters she thinks she's barren. So bring in God. Her God, not mine. Ann isn't in my congregation any more. All her talk is absolutes. I suppose that comes of going for long walks on your own . . . . . (*Pause*)

MOSCROP. I'll do my best.

SCADDING. I know you will. Which leaves a single problem. Who will do it? (*Pause*. MOSCROP *looks at* SCADDING *with an expression of horror*) Not you, silly.

MOSCROP. God, man, I am not fit to ask!

SCADDING. It's a funny thing. You would think, wouldn't you, a man who held the highest office in the land, who had a reputation—if not as a fox, as something of a fixer—could lay his hand, could roll up his sleeve and dip down in the bottomless sump of government to find and finger individuals to do a little thing like this. When I had millions at my beck, had the authority to poison, snipe and what, in my retirement cannot find one spare murderer. I do think that's funny, do you? How do you get a murderer? I am as in the dark on this as any cuckolded sales-man. (MOSCROP *is staring at him*) I'm sorry if I shock you, John. I sometimes wonder why I'm lonely. But I know really. It's because I never condescend to horror. I lay my thoughts down naked. Of course I look a brute. But I'm not vain of my brutality. I think if I were vain of it, then I would sin.

MOSCROP. Too deep for me.

SCADDING. Never, you supple priest.

MOSCROP. Supple?

SCADDING. Supple, yes.

MOSCROP. You don't mean subtle?

SCADDING. No. I mean your hips move, don't they? Up and down? Not a burden in the bed, like me? Not supine for a woman? (MOSCROP *looks at him.* SCADDING *starts to go again*) They could put a pin in mine. Some shaft of stainless steel in all the crumbling pelvic mess. But I'm in terror of the specialists. For all their oaths they might maim me under the anaesthetic. (*He moves on*)

MOSCROP. I think I have to say—(SCADDING *stops*) All life is precious in the eyes of God.

SCADDING. But not in the eyes of man, I think. I doubt if a more useless scrap of inbred flesh was ever spewed out of the English aristocracy. And you know I rather like him.

He goes out. MOSCROP *watches the door for some moments.*

MOSCROP. **Why am I not a bishop!**

Pause. He trembles with suppressed rage, then goes out. After some time, YOUNG BEVIN *comes in, pushing his wife in front of him. She sits, head hanging, in a pew.*

YOUNG BEVIN. Yar thar are yar? (*He walks a little way up the aisle*) Alloa thar!

LANA. Not doin' it, Gary! Not doin' it!

YOUNG BEVIN. **Where are yar!**

LANA. God punish us, won't 'un? God strike us 'ard!

YOUNG BEVIN. Thass wha' us askin', thass wha' us fin'in' out, b'ain't us, silly cow? If there was sum fuckin' vicar in the place! Sun'y fuckin' mornin', b'ain't it? **'Ulloa thar!** (MOSCROP *appears, dragging a surplice over his shoulders*)

MOSCROP. I am giving service here.

YOUNG BEVIN. I b'aint be 'ere for service, Mr Moscrop.

MOSCROP. Bevin, isn't it? Bevin the Younger?

YOUNG BEVIN. S'me, right enough.

MOSCROP. Of Cholera Cottage, Ricketts Lane, in the parish of Incest? Bevin of the transistor and the Buick?

YOUNG BEVIN. Chevrolet . . .

MOSCROP. The whispering of malnutrition . . . the rasp of Johnny Cash . . . .

YOUNG BEVIN. Won't keep tha, Mr Moscrop.

MOSCROP. Good.

YOUNG BEVIN. Tell Lana 'ow she mus' 'ave operation. Tell 'ar. Stick in 'er noddle t'ain't no sin. Fuckin' tired 'a prattle. S'na my kid neither. Tell 'ar, thun. (*He sits down, waits*)

MOSCROP. Do I understand that you are pregnant?

LANA. Reckon.

YOUNG BEVIN. Nine time, fuckin' 'ell!

MOSCROP. God blesses you. In abundance.

LANA (*to* BEVIN). See!

YOUNG BEVIN. **Dar'n fuckin' encourage 'ar! Tha's fuckin' leads 'ar on, thar' barmy turd!**

LANA. Abundant! Says so, don' 'ee!

MOSCROP. Pink in the wet pink, life squirming through the blizzard, through nicotine, through drug. Vile thing, life. Weeds will up, even in Hiroshima . . .

YOUNG BEVIN. B'ain't bin no bastard under my roof yet, nor gonna be, by Christ, no squealin' tit-sucker as Ar've not shot in yar!

LANA. God blesses me, so thar!

YOUNG BEVIN. Wi' wha'! Wi! loony spunk? Sum fuckin'blessin', tha'!

MOSCROP. Who is the father of your child?

LANA. Dunno.

YOUNG BEVIN. Do fuckin' know, tha' does!

LANA. **Dunno, so thar!**

YOUNG BEVIN. 'as fuckin' good idea, thun! Put lug'ole to 'ar navel, s'na Devon fuckin' local, tell 'ee tha'! S'more fuckin' Knightsbridge!

MOSCROP. I have service in one minute.

YOUNG BEVIN. S'long enough. Tell 'ar God says eight's enough.

MOSCROP (*to* LANA). What's your name?

LANA. Lana.

MOSCROP. Lana. All right, Lana. Now tell me honestly, do you think your husband may not be the father of your child?

YOUNG BEVIN. S'na bloody child. Stop callin' it a child!

LANA. What is it, thun?

YOUNG BEVIN. S'a tadpole.

MOSCROP. Just answer the question. (*Pause. She shrugs*)

LANA. May nart. Then 'gain, may be.

YOUNG BEVIN. A'n't bin near tha' six months—

LANA. 'ave.

YOUNG BEVIN. **'A'n't bin! Wha' tha' saying'? Started fuckin' in ma sleep?**

HEYDAY *appears in the door. Pause.*

HEYDAY. Am I early?

YOUNG BEVIN. Missus, A'll not feed an' clothe the barmy's bastard. Fact.

Pause. HEYDAY *looks from* MOSCROP *to* LANA, *to* BEVIN. LANA *suddenly weeps.*

HEYDAY (*to* MOSCROP). You haven't put the hymns up.

MOSCROP. No.

HEYDAY. Do, then. (MOSCROP *goes to the hymn-board. Puts up number cards*) We specifically asked you, didn't we, to take the pill.

LANA. Yes, mum.

HEYDAY. What happened, then?

LANA. Fargart.

YOUNG BEVIN. **Fargart! Lost 'em, Didn't tha'?**

LANA. Lost 'em.

YOUNG BEVIN. Fuckin' darg ran off wi' 'um. Told tha' keep soddin' pills where darg can't get, told tha', didn't A? Stupid bitch, can't keep tha mind on nothin'!

LANA. **Got nine kids, a'n't I?**

YOUNG BEVIN. **Eight. Gart eight.** (*He turns to go*) Tell 'ar, s'pig pen if she keeps dam' thing, so thar! (*He clumps out the church*)

LANA. Sin tar kill a baby.

HEYDAY. Yes and no.

LANA. Mum?

HEYDAY. Worse than contraception, is it? Little bit of latex
rubber all the difference between sin and innocence?

LANA. Darn know . . .

HEYDAY. Funny God that would be. Not one I'd worship.

LANA. Darn know . . . .

HEYDAY. You must decide, though. Only you. (*Pause*)

LANA. S'nart only me, though, is it?

HEYDAY. I'll take care of Bevin.

LANA. Nart Bevin. Fuck 'un. 'S'ma af'ernoons at Manor pays
for Chevvy, don't 'un?

HEYDAY. Who, then?

LANA. Him. (*Pause*)

HEYDAY. He knows? **He** knows?

LANA. Told 'un. Slipped out, see? (*Pause*)

HEYDAY. Go home, Lana. We are late for service.

LANA. Yes, mum. (*She starts to go, stops*) 'E were that pleased,
poor man! (*She goes out*)

HEYDAY. Fuck.

MOSCROP. Yes. (*Pause*) The organist is here.

HEYDAY. My fault this. I got her for him. Out of the goodness
of my heart. For charity. And look! I am full of decent
motive and I get slapped. What have I done? I have offended
something. Something wants to wound me. Cocky's here.

MOSCROP. Of the Daily World filfth?

HEYDAY. He says coincidence but I say the walls are closing in.
Help me, John.

MOSCROP. I want to help you. Darling one. Want to. Love, love—
Not yet Mr Ducker! (*The organ stops*) What does he look like?

HEYDAY. Ugly.

MOSCROP. With a big nose?

HEYDAY. For his job.

MOSCROP. Then he came here this morning. Said he'd heard
Lucky screaming in the night. I told him the St Leger myth.
He has a boy with him. A maniac with tattooed arms.

HEYDAY. All I want to do is rest now. Want to make myself
again. But I am being hounded down.

MOSCROP. Only Cocky.

HEYDAY. Spirits.

MOSCROP. Not spirits, no.

HEYDAY. Yes! Spirits! Christ in his anger, I don't know what—
(*The organ starts again*)

MOSCROP. **All right, Ducker!** (*It stops*) Christ, I want to—want
to—

HEYDAY. Start, will you? Start. (MOSCROP *goes to the altar steps, takes up his hymn book*)

MOSCROP. We begin our service this Sunday with hymn number 775, 'Rise up, Rejoice and Glorify!'

The organ begins an introduction.

HEYDAY. Roy says we have to murder him.
MOSCROP. Oh?
HEYDAY. Lucky.
MOSCROP. Oh?
HEYDAY. What do we do? (MOSCROP *goes towards her*) Roy has this— (*He puts out a hand towards her*) Roy is, you see— (*He holds her shoulders*) Is always right— (*He kisses her waist, her hips*) No . . . . This is not helping me!

DUCKER'S *voice is heard over the organ, singing hymn no 775. Fade to black.*

Scene Four

A bedroom in the Beggar's Arms. DOWNCHILD *is in bed.* STOAT *sits at the foot.*

DOWNCHILD. The vicar says there's a ghost. There is no ghost. Heyday says she's innocent. She's guilty. The publican calls this a bed. It's a death trap. I've never been to bed before and exposed myself to tetanus. Was there ever such a spate of lying? It's endemic to the place. Now Stoat declares he loves me, when he can't do.
STOAT. I said I'm sorry 'bout the beach.
DOWNCHILD. The beach? The beach! What beach? The beach does not exist. There is no beach. I say you cannot love me. I say it as a simple fact. I dazzle you, but that's not love. What have beaches got to do with it? (*Pause*)
STOAT. You make it 'ard, Tom.
DOWNCHILD. What?
STOAT. **I dunno but yer make it 'ard!** (*Pause*) Sometimes I wonder if I like yer.
DOWNCHILD. Dear boy, I'm sure you don't. (*Pause*)
STOAT. Wha'?
DOWNCHILD. Not like, nor love. You are just a baby, wandering in the great big noisy fairground of my character. Bumping and bewildered. Eyes big in the lightshow. Ears singing in the music. You call it love because the word exists. You think it does you honour. Please don't bother. The only person who could love me I could never love. Do you understand that? Does that penetrate your fog? (*Pause*)
STOAT. Why are we 'ere, then?
DOWNCHILD. Because I picked you out, that's why. Plucked you

from your poverty, thrilled by some little turning of the hip, some little twitch not common to every desecrator of the tower-block, some orthopaedic eccentricity that excited me, that's why. For that one twitch I rescued you from rowdy wretchedness, from kicking mongrels over commons, throwing stones at lovers, and the sopping knicker in the back seat of the bus, you pimply nothing, you factory fodder, shot out of some hag's belly following a drunken fuck . . . .

STOAT. Yer turnin' yerself on again . . .

DOWNCHILD. Where would you be if I'd not found you? Squirming on the pavement with a lewd gob full of fish and chips? Oh, dirty little life! For all your chains and leather, coloured hair and strut, I never saw a less valued or more spewed on bit of flesh . . . dear boy . . .

STOAT. I am not coming back to bed.

DOWNCHILD. This thing that shrugged itself into maturity in the reign of Ann and Roy, that heaved itself up in some tele-screaming squalor while they fucked to Big Ben's chimes . . .

STOAT. Give us me Y-fronts.

DOWNCHILD. Come here.

STOAT. Fuckin' not!

DOWNCHILD. **Come on!** (STOAT *grabs his clothes together, sweeps out of the room, slamming the door. Pause.* DOWNCHILD *is very still, then at last, gets out of bed, starts to dress*) It's a wonderful thing to be a socialist. A socialist by instinct. Red, as it were, in the blood. For all my breeding and the slight retch in my gizzard at the odour of the housemaid's flesh, it triumphed over me, the naughty bacillus, I was a convert to the working man. It was the sunshine did it, making the noisy road men strip. The white backed Irish labourer. Sneaked behind the curtain I gasped to watch him stoop. Surplus value. Surplus love. (SCADDING *enters. Pause*)

SCADDING. Let myself in.

DOWNCHILD. I hate knocking. There's no dignity in it. (*He begins brushing his hair.* SCADDING *sits*)

SCADDING. How's the boss?

DOWNCHILD. Dying, I think. Something's gnawing his bladder.

SCADDING. Good.

DOWNCHILD. It's the fate of Fleet Street editors. I've long held the belief that all cancer comes from contradiction. It's the disease of the age. All this lying has to have a penalty.

SCADDING. Your health is robust, is it?

DOWNCHILD. Luscious. I'm in luscious health. I don't think we've ever met, have we? I'm Tom Downchild. I stood for Yeovil East in '50. As a Communist. (*His hand is extended.* SCADDING *doesn't take it*)

SCADDING. You have a very funny job.

DOWNCHILD. There's nothing funny about writing novels, Sir Roy.

It's all pain.

SCADDING. I meant the Cocky Column.

DOWNCHILD. That's not a job, that's a hobby. It's pure
coincidence the hobby yields more money.

SCADDING. Funny because useless.

DOWNCHILD. Oh, don't say that! There's nothing useless in
relating misdemeanours. Debs' adulteries make fascinating
reading on the 8.17 from Surbiton to Waterloo. Gives meaning
to the lives of clerks, colour to a typist's dreams. Crumbs of
the foul feast. Makes them paw the window of the house of
sin. But you didn't come here to natter ethics.

SCADDING. Ethics? No, I never do.

DOWNCHILD. Quite so. Which tie goes best with cream?
(*He holds a couple against his shirt*)

SCADDING. Lady Heyday is a friend of mine.

DOWNCHILD. This one?

SCADDING. A dear friend. Interpret that in any way you wish.

DOWNCHILD. No, this . . . (*He starts tying it*)

SCADDING. She's ill.

DOWNCHILD (*stops*). Ah. And walking the cliffs at midnight
is in obedience to doctor's orders, I suppose?

SCADDING. She sleeps badly. Has to wear a mask to keep the
starlight out her eyes . . .

DOWNCHILD. I don't think I ever realized, until I was Sir Cocky,
how dire the health of all our rulers is, crawling from restaurant
to club as pale as death, it's enough to make you grieve.
Whenever I'm begged off, it's always for the sake of someone's
health. I must be a virus or a germ, flinging them on their backs
like this. Fortunately for the public I am without a conscience,
save all my money for the RSPCA. (*Pause*)

SCADDING. I gave away my power. Influence I kept.

DOWNCHILD. There is a trinity of warnings and appeals in this.
Goes—pity, influence, and violence—in that order. I'm only
waiting for you to say you know of half-a-dozen guardsmen
wouldn't say no to drilling on my fingers.

SCADDING. I don't know any guardsmen. I suggest guardsmen's
more your cup of tea.

DOWNCHILD. Sir Roy, touché! (*He slips on a jacket, picks up
some sunglasses, turns to leave*) They tell me there's a ghost
here. I won't have it. The only ghost round here is you. (*He
leaves the room.* SCADDING *looks around him*)

SCADDING. The smell of bed. Of bad, bent love. (*He pokes in the
sheets with his stick, takes out* STOAT'S *Y-fronts on the end*)
Human soup . . . . (STOAT *comes in*)

STOAT. My pants.

SCADDING *passes them to him. He bundles them into a bag along
with other items.* SCADDING *watches.*

SCADDING. Not stopping, then?

STOAT. Got pride. Got little thing called dignity. Me. Even me. Been pissed on six months, slagged by screws, but still the little flower grows. Will bloom, won't it? In dung even?

SCADDING. Done time, have you?

STOAT. Encyclopaedia, C to D. (*He tosses it in*)

SCADDING. Grievous, was it? Your particular deed?

STOAT. Not so very. Not so grievous with the carver 'as what 'e sticks on with 'is gob. That's woundin', too. Draws blood.

SCADDING. But was it?

STOAT. What? (*Pause*)

SCADDING. Grievous?

STOAT (*stops packing, looks at* SCADDING). 'O are you?

SCADDING. My face is slipping out of the collective memory, I see.

STOAT. I don't mean 'o are you. I know 'o you are. I mean 'o are you?

SCADDING. Wandered in.

STOAT. Like pussy? Saw the winder open, must come through?

SCADDING. What's prison like nowadays?

STOAT. Ecstasy.

SCADDING. Meet killers much?

STOAT. **Look, 'o are you!** (*He stares at* SCADDING, *horribly*) Chancin', ain't yer? Ditherin' in a bedroom with a fierce flash fruit like me? Could roll yer an' lift the roof off Wan'sworth with the cheering when it broke the news. Tier on tier of chanting con, 'The Stoat! The Stoat!' in gorgeous monotony. I ain't forgot yer walking stick. Left its little kiss on me. (*He thrusts the top of his head towards* SCADDING. *Pause*)

SCADDING. Do me a murder. Quick. Before you go. (*Pause*)

STOAT. Wha'?

SCADDING. Nothing. (*He gets up, starts to leave*)

STOAT. Wha'? (*He stops, without turning*)

SCADDING. Does he love you?

STOAT. Love?

SCADDING. Is he three-quarters barmy over you?

STOAT. We suffer.

SCADDING. That's all I need to know.

He goes out. STOAT *zips up his bag, looks round, follows him. The lights dim.*

Scene Five

Night. DOWNCHILD *switches on the light.* OLD BEVIN *comes in, gawps around him.*

OLD BEVIN. 'S'tarp suite you'ave, thun? Christ, t'is luxury! Ol' Jack ain't let this room since end o' war, nor dust it neither, looks

to me! (*He laughs, looks at the bed*) Cud na swear to sheets, 'im
don't change 'em more 'un needs to, fucked if I'd kip 'ere, got
itchin' much? I won't sit down, thank 'ee. Christ, Jack, thou robber,
thou rascal! (*He chuckles*)

DOWNCHILD. The room-service is legendary. Have a drink, will you?

OLD BEVIN. Thank 'ee, thank 'ee, sor.

DOWNCHILD (*pouring a mugful*). You were telling me about your
son.

OLD BEVIN. Gary?

DOWNCHILD. Yes. Do you have another?

OLD BEVIN. Only Gary.

DOWNCHILD. Excellent. He must be the one.

OLD BEVIN. Look at tha, ceilin'! Got tar drip on thee!

DOWNCHILD. It hasn't rained yet.

OLD BEVIN. Tha's sky I see!

DOWNCHILD. More than likely.

OLD BEVIN. You pay for this? Or does 'e pay thee? (*He slaps his
knee*) Jack's a darg! 'e is a darg, though? B'ain't 'e?

DOWNCHILD. A dog if I ever saw one. Gary drives a Chevrolet
with eight children in the back.

OLD BEVIN. 'E loves a motor, Gary does. Up'olstery's impala.
'as quadrophonic, an' goat mats on the floor.

DOWNCHILD. Quite an achievement, on a labourer's wage.

OLD BEVIN (*pointing*). Tha' bit o' carpet! Knew I seen it sum place!
T'was on floor o' chicken run lass week, I swear to Gard!
(*He laughs*) Jack's a darg!

DOWNCHILD. This year's registration Chevrolet. On fifty-seven
pounds a week?

OLD BEVIN (*slamming down the mug*). Christ, gart to take my turn
at arrers, gart team from Cat an' Piddle 'ere tonight!

DOWNCHILD. **How does he do it, Ted?** (*Pause. BEVIN looks
steadily at him*)

OLD BEVIN. 'ad squire 'ere not five year ago. Right cunt St Leger.
Would na run drinkin' water to the cottages. T'was all fat arse and
'eadscarf. Fuck tha'. Us wanted Arab Sheikh to buy up place.
Bring money in. Servants an' like. Dun take no change out fiver,
dun no Arab, see? (*Pause*) Got no sheikh, did us? Got wiggle
arsin' ladyship. But she dun nart to 'urt us, see? Put water in.
An' colour tele in tied cottages. Fuck if we care who fucks whose
arse up thar. (*Pause*) Lay arf, all right? Am tellin' thee. (*He goes
out. DOWNCHILD does not move for a long time. He sniffs.*)

DOWNCHILD. Stink of peasant. (*He sniffs*) Stink of old man
never washed. (*He sniffs*) Old crutch. (*He sniffs*) Old piss. (*He
sniffs*) Stoat odour very weak. (*He sniffs*) My perspiring boy.
(*He sniffs urgently*) Can't find him in the old man's blitz!
(*He goes to the bed, inhales a sheet*) Gone cold! His scent!
(*He looks round desperately*) Encyclopaedia! (*He rips out the
drawers of a dressing-table*) **Encyclopaedia!** (*With a howl*

*of despair he drops to his knees, sobs, rocks to and fro. Suddenly
he stops, gets to his feet. Pause)* Five years and you'll be pissing
through a catheter. Ga-ga on the sea-front. Nasty odour through
the tartan blanket. **Get a bit of dignity!**

Scene Six

The manor. An OLD WOMAN *asleep in a chair.* HEYDAY *enters.*

HEYDAY. Mum. (*Pause*) Mum. (*Pause*) Put your knees together.
   (*Pause*) Hag.

She goes out again. DICKER *enters, in a dressing gown. He takes a
seat, crosses his legs, waits.* HEYDAY *and* SCADDING *enter.*
HEYDAY *closes the door.* SCADDING *looks at* DICKER.

SCADDING. Well, Lucky.
HEYDAY. I'll say it.
SCADDING. I will. I will because I thought of it. Because I am
   the instigator. The prime-mover, if you like. (*Pause*) Lucky,
   you've become impossible.
DICKER. Yes.
SCADDING. We don't know what to do with you.
DICKER. No.
SCADDING. It's the madness, isn't it?
DICKER. Yes.
SCADDING. Which you feared. Which your father laid in you.
   Which came curled up in his genes. A maggot, or an egg.
DICKER. Quite.
SCADDING. Which hatched. And then began to crawl.
DICKER. Yes.
SCADDING. Across your brain.
DICKER. Yes.
SCADDING. Madness which pops up as surely as the family
   nose. About the early forties, all Lord Dickers are transported
   to their tombs. For tombs read padded cells in exclusive
   nursing-homes.
DICKER. Yes.
SCADDING. To shout their last years out unheard. To the tinkle
   of some hundred guineas every week. Behind the cedars and
   the lawns.
DICKER. Yes.
SCADDING. Dread.
DICKER. Quite.
SCADDING. Awful dread. (*Pause*)
HEYDAY. I think—
SCADDING. Let me finish—
HEYDAY. I think we're—

SCADDING. I will finish, Ann. *(He walks a little, stops)* Luckily, where's
   the dignity in that? You said your governor smeared his room with
   shit.
DICKER. He did.
SCADDING. I think, Lucky, you would do well to miss all that . . .
   Now things are crumbling and the signs are there for all to
   see . . . . *(Pause)* Do well to say thus far and no further. *(Pause)*
   Courage. And genuine nobility. *(Pause)*
DICKER. I'm a catholic. *(Pause. HEYDAY and SCADDING exchange
   looks)*
HEYDAY. Never told us that, Lucky.
DICKER. Only just remembered it. (SCADDING *gives a nod to*
   HEYDAY, *who goes out*)
SCADDING. Lovely for the Pope, eh? These injunctions? But the
   Pope's not going barmy. Can you see him smearing the Vatican
   with shit? Flinging his turds at the Michaelangelos? Tossing in
   his mitre? I think there'd be a change of heart if his holiness
   got up to tricks like that. Be a shower of encyclicals, bulls, edicts,
   Christ knows what. Lucky, love thyself. If we didn't love you,
   would we have come up with this?
HEYDAY *(returning with a sherry-glass of yellow liquid)*. For
   God's sake, Roy!
SCADDING. It's because we love him we do this!
DICKER. Thank you, yes *(Pause)*
SCADDING. What Ann's got there, Lucky, is a drink. I am
   assured it tastes good. Like egg-flip. Do you like egg-flip?
DICKER. No.
SCADDING. Put a cherry in it, shall we? *(He takes the glass from
   HEYDAY, goes towards DICKER)*
DICKER. The governor said, when I was tiny, when I was six,
   come in the great hall and read to me what it says under the
   family crest, a shield this is, supported by twin griffin, slashed
   sinister with seven bezants on a field of blood, and I read in my
   childish voice, Do What You Will. **Do what you will,** he boomed,
   typical governor, shook the Doric columns of Italian marble,
   scared the pigeons off the roof. There are others, he said, like
   I serve, but ours is **Do what you will.** *(Pause)* And now, in my
   best years, I find I cannot. I could kick his coffin through the
   mausoleum gates . . . . *(Pause)*
SCADDING. We love you, Lucky.

HEYDAY *turns away.* SCADDING *hands* DICKER *the drink.*
He takes it, swirls it round. Pause.

DICKER. I can't.
SCADDING. Try.
DICKER. I have a boy, you see. *(Pause)*
SCADDING. A boy. You mean a girl?
DICKER. I mean a boy.

SCADDING. The Right Honourable Jasmine? At the Lycée?

DICKER. A boy, I said. (*Pause*)

SCADDING. Where?

DICKER. In his mother's tummy. (SCADDING *looks at* HEYDAY)

SCADDING. Ann and I will make ourselves responsible for him.

DICKER. Boy needs a father.

SCADDING. I will be his father.

DICKER. Yes, but—

SCADDING. **What bloody use are you?** (*Pause.* LUCKY *still stares into the drink, still swirls it round in the glass*) Sorry. (*Pause*) But this is such a good idea.

DICKER. Very grateful.

SCADDING. Drink it, then.

Pause. DICKER *stands up, swirling the drink still. Suddenly he drops it on the floor. Pause.*

DICKER. Whoops. (*Pause.* SCADDING *looks darkly at him*)

SCADDING. Prefers to be a human mess.

DICKER. I think so, yes. (*He shrugs*) Sorry. (*He goes out the room. Pause*)

HEYDAY. Roy. I should be sick. And sick. And sick. Why aren't I sick?

SCADDING. Not stopping you.

HEYDAY. Ugly moment in an ugly life. Want to be sick!

SCADDING. Spew, then. Go on. Spew.

HEYDAY. I can't!

SCADDING. She can't. Do I vomit? Do I make a dance of it? I don't. I swallow. Down bile. Down dinner. I eat up your reproaches. Yum, yum. Stick your conscience on my plate, I am the brute, cry your tear drops in my glass, I drink all, I am the man who does, whose back is big enough for every stick, for every thrashing by the squeamish or the rank cowardly! Take your principles to market son, put your ideals in the scales!

HEYDAY. You are not in cabinet.

SCADDING. Cabinet is life. Life's cabinet. (*He kicks* MRS HEYDAY *gently on the shin*) Wake up, mum, get us a drink. (*She stirs*)

MOLLY. I was dreamin' I was being fucked . . .

SCADDING. What do you expect, the real thing? Come on, Molly, give us all a scotch.

MOLLY (*to* HEYDAY). By yer father, on a rock. With water sloppin' round us . . . .

SCADDING. This is the mobile library . . . .

MOLLY. I could feel 'im . . . . Really feel 'im up me, Ann . . . (*They look at her*) Funny, 'cos 'e would never do it out of bed. I wanted 'im to. Do it in the open. Like the beasts. (*Pause*) Never asked 'im. (*Pause*) Stupid. (*She gets up, goes to pour the drinks*)

SCADDING. Life won't be stifled, will it? Even when the arguments are overwhelmingly in favour of it. Molly dreams of fucking. Lucky clings to—what? I believe he tried, too. Now we shall have to bring in someone else.

HEYDAY. No.

SCADDING. Logic, Ann.

HEYDAY. I am not standing by and—

SCADDING. Logic, logic, for fuck's sake!

HEYDAY. We lived by logic, governed by it! Hateful, dead thing!

MOLLY. Silly . . . .

HEYDAY. Do not dare to call me silly.

SCADDING. Ann, your beauty in my eyes has always been that there wasn't much in you, if I might say so, that you could call feminine. You look like a woman. You have the body of one. But I was glad to think I had the best of both worlds. I had skirt and everything that comes with it; but with your pants on I could have been ranting with a bloke.

HEYDAY. Wonderful mutation.

SCADDING. It was paradise. But lately—what? The sea air, is it? She will neither think nor fuck. Come over violently feminine.

MOLLY. Roy—

SCADDING. Fact, Molly. Fact.

HEYDAY. Yes.

SCADDING. I say this, in the presence of Molly, because—

MOLLY. I don't mind.

SCADDING. She doesn't mind because—

MOLLY. What's true is true—

SCADDING. Thank you, because you know as well as I do Lucky's got to go, and I'd appreciate a little backing, the backing I'm accustomed to, less reference to feeling sick, let's be sick by all means, but after. (*Pause*) And now I sound a brute. (*He swallows his drink*) Thus brutes are made. The sheep who stands its ground becomes a monster. (*He goes out. Pause*)

MOLLY. You aren't nice to 'im. I tell you whether you wanna know or not. You aren't nice to 'im.

HEYDAY. You be nice. Perhaps he'll sleep with you.

MOLLY. Disgusting.

HEYDAY. Your knees are ever drifting open. Casting cruel lights up thighs.

MOLLY. I'm old. I fall asleep.

HEYDAY. Wear longer skirts.

MOLLY. What is this?

HEYDAY. Just hating you.

MOLLY. You're tired.

HEYDAY. All the damage. All the silly business with my cunt. A vile life. Thanks to you.

MOLLY. More tired than you realize.

HEYDAY. A poke for delegates. Up against the tea-urn at the party conferences. Head down in the back of cars. In Blackpool bedrooms got the soil of honest labour in my crutch. The blonde lad. The lad who fucks.

MOLLY. Did well, Ann.

HEYDAY. Somewhat imperfect English arse, but was planning to attend to that. With two short incisions in the dorsal pelvic muscle surgeons can raise it, make it high and rather French. Won't win equestrian rosettes, but prefer. Call it Parisienne Shape D.

MOLLY. Nothing wrong with your bum. Same as mine.

HEYDAY. Was booked into the clinic when the snap election came along. The specialist incidentally, had a hair lip. As for the thread veins in my thigh—

MOLLY. Every woman 'as—

HEYDAY. **The thread veins in my thighs**—these are hereditary, from our dead docker of a dad, working his vengeance from beyond the grave, and are treatable by electrolysis, the same scientific blessing that withered my stray pubic hair—

MOLLY. Don't see why you 'ad to—

HEYDAY. Spent hour after hour on a couch, on sterile paper while a humming thing improved my crutch—

MOLLY. Didn't 'ave to—

HEYDAY. **My toilet has been half my life!** (*Pause*) But I was beautiful. How else, when Oxford intellectuals with rumpled hair and sagging tights, slack-titted women descended from the aristocracy of English pacifists, spouted their breathless wisdom in the cabinet, how else could I govern them? Me from Catford? Me who only took the notes? (*Pause*) Roy is a little man. Bought me chocolate liquers every week and took them from between my breasts . . . . (*Pause*) Does it go? The feel for sex? (MOLLY *shakes her head*) Horrifying. (*She turns to leave the room*)

MOLLY. The roses.

HEYDAY (*stops*). What?

MOLLY (*looking out the window*). Roses. Roses far as I can see . . . .

HEYDAY. Yes?

MOLLY. That ol' dead docker . . . . couldn't get a bean shoot up in Catford . . . with the fumes . . . . .

(*Pause.* HEYDAY *goes out. Fade to black*)

ACT TWO

Scene One

The field at night. STOAT *is standing in the hay. Sounds of the country.*

STOAT. Litt'l footpath—over stile—near 'azel wood—catch light'ouse
beam—fingers freezin'—whatcha doin'—gone stiff, 'ave yer—August
is it—call this summer—Christ almighty—'ot and randy, ain't it—
August—quick little daggers—frozen solid—no pockets in these
fuckin' jeans—down me front then—my last 'ot spot—thawed out
in the sweaty briefs—this is right, is it—**whass'at!**—litt'l footpath—
over stile—near 'azel wood—catch light'ouse beam—jump out on 'im
—flash in the wheat—knee on windpipe—stifle screams—**whass'at**—
bird flocks in the bum of night—'ullo, fingers—can't 'ave this—
be nimble with a full grown knob— **whass'at I said!**—cow is it—
cow, is that—the noises 'ere—the racket—do badgers attack in
packs—snakes bite yer feet—this is the litt'el footpath is it—near
'azel wood—in light'ouse beam—if this is silence—give us Vaux'all—
this ain't night—night's orange lights—night's blue bulbs on the
landin'—**sumthin's bit me! Blood-suckin' bat!**

He ducks down in the wheat. DICKER *appears, stands still, gazing
into the sea. He speaks with level calm.*

DICKER. Would greatly appreciate refrain from fucking on my
yacht. The dago fingers on my wife, accept that, naturally. The
dago suit, the dago socks. But in my cabin, nudging her flap of tit
and doing dago grunting, I resent. I know he is not trash, I know he
is a kind of prince, has got a villa up some Tuscan mountain but—
come here that gull! (*He stares into the night sky*) **Yes, you!. You!
No, not you! The one with the beak!** (*Pause. He is level again*) Nip
down to Malta, will you, there's a good gull, and shit the port-hole
window with my name, tell them I am not lying in some scrub, not
under gorse, write **Lucky Lives and Lucky Thrives.** And if it's open
to the dago air, nip through and peck her nipple off, the dirty
brown old nipple, bring it back. Thank you. (*Pause, then he starts
to move off. He stops, suddenly. Pause*) Erm. (*Pause*) Now erm.
(*Pause*) You see I have these nostrils, which along with lunacy,
have been handed down to me, nostrils which are the acme of
efficiency, the one perfection in the Dicker Hereditary Mess.
(*Pause*) I mean to say I smell you. (*Pause*) Have you come to hit
me on the head? (*Pause, then* STOAT *rises out of the wheat, behind*

him.)

STOAT. Be good now, eh? Stand still.

DICKER (*not turning*). Yes.

STOAT. Because I never done this.

DICKER. Ah.

STOAT. Not cold. Done it in a flash of course. Done it boilin', but—
(*Pause*) My fingers are like fuckin' ice. (*He is fumbling with a
blade*)

DICKER. Can I help—

STOAT. **Shuddup!** (*He is struggling now, shaking*)

DICKER. What's the trouble?

STOAT. **Fuck, oh fuck!** (*He chucks the blade far away.*
DICKER *turns, looks at him. Pause*)

DICKER. Ever been in Pirbright? Guards depot? (STOAT *shakes
his head*) Seem to recognize the face. The phizog under cap and
badge.

STOAT. Nope.

DICKER. All squaddies' phizogs are identical, they say. Ring of
pimples crowned by cold on lip . . . . (*Pause*) Are you in the pay
of Roy? (STOAT *nods*) Roy says I am the dead class. He says in
one hundred years they will not understand how I was permitted
to exist. I say in one hundred years they will not understand how
you were, either.

STOAT. What are yer?

DICKER. I am a peer.

STOAT. What's peers do?

DICKER. Got a red seat in the chamber.

STOAT. Chamber?

DICKER. Yes.

STOAT. That's it, is it? Ain't nothin' else?

DICKER. Stood in the turret of a saracen. Once carried a goblet for the
Queen. Or Mother, was it? Anyway, was a cup-bearer to some fart
once. And gambled. (*Pause*) Gambled, gambled, fucked and gambled.
(*Pause*) What's your name?

STOAT. Forgot.

DICKER. Orphan, are you?

STOAT. By inclination. So would you be if you seen my mum. (*Pause.*
DICKER *extends a hand*)

DICKER. Shake hands. (STOAT *shakes his hand*) **That's nice.** (*He
holds it, shaking it*) That's jolly nice . . .

DOWNCHILD (*appearing out the wheat*). I have to come in here.
Someone will say Tom Downchild is a snooper and I would not
carry that curse to the grave with me.

STOAT. Well, what the fuck are—

DOWNCHILD. Silence, Stoat. If I don't own you, you're not here.
You have no existence. You are a figment of my brain.

STOAT. I don't 'ave ter—

DOWNCHILD. I imagined you elsewhere by now. I imagined you

spreadeagled on a roundabout. Under a lorry driver. So be there.

DICKER. Who is this?

DOWNCHILD. Well, you of all this rural set should know me. I had
your sister's aborted honeymoon on the public breakfast table
before Prince Ali's 97th piece of luggage was back on the plane.
Charlotte's Shame Shook Sheikh. A half-title I treasure to this day.
Pity she had to hack her wrists, but the inclination to spill blood
runs in the family. Like the profusion of its bastards.

DICKER. Muckballs of the Daily World.

DOWNCHILD. And they say there are detectives in Rio after you.
Well, it proves my theory that no great artist can enjoy a holiday!
And I was hoping to complete the fourth volume of my trilogy.
I must say, though, I confess it outright to the moon and stars,
you are a whale, Lucky, when I was fishing for a cod at best.
It puts a strain on my rod, I can tell you.

STOAT. 'o is 'e?

DOWNCHILD. Who is he, he says. Bewilderment puts beauty in that
mean gob . . . who do you think he is? St Leger's ghost?

*There is a sudden and sinister cry off, a howl of pain oddly distorted
and amplified.*

STOAT (*with an involuntary cry*). **Whass'at!**

ST LEGER. ST LEG–ER AND ENG–LAND HO!

STOAT. Christ!

DOWNCHILD. Stoat!

STOAT. **Oh, fuck!** (*The moon is obscured by clouds, thowing the stage
into darkness*) **He–lp!** (*He charges off into the night, accompanied
by* DICKER)

DOWNCHILD. Come back you—

ST LEGER. **Oh, there's the en–em–y!**

DOWNCHILD. It's just another—just another—just—some bloody
English racket—Stoat— (*He shudders, but does not give ground, his
eyes tight shut.* ST LEGER *appears, waving a sword under*
DOWNCHILD'S *nose*) Moon.

ST LEGER. **St Leg–er and Eng–land, ho!**

DOWNCHILD. **Moon! Moon!** (*The moon comes out again.*
DOWNCHILD *opens his eyes, sees* ST LEGER *standing before him
with a loud-hailer. Pause*) You look gorgeous, vicar, but the shoulder-
strap goes underneath the epaulette . . . . (ST LEGER *makes no reply.
From the shadows, the* BEVINS *appear, stand menacingly*) The
yeomen of old England . . . . Who needs to pull a bow-string when
there's fruit machines? (*Pause*) If you're going to beat me, make it
passionate, please . . .

YOUNG BEVIN. Too much fockin' gab, mister.

DOWNCHILD. Funny vanity I had once, vicar . . . that with command
of English I could chatter malice out of anyone, flatter dogs out
of biting. It's a fallacy of course. (YOUNG BEVIN *takes a step
towards him*) I must warn you, I have been laid into by some proper

experts in my time . . . though never under a moon like this . . .
(*The* BEVINS *move closer*) Oh, fuck all of you . . . . (*He
collapses. They stare at him*)
OLD BEVIN. Garn fainted on us, bent bugger.
YOUNG BEVIN. Shove fence pole up us bum.
OLD BEVIN. Pick 'un up, will 'ee?
YOUNG BEVIN. Thistle in 'us arse'ole—
MOSCROP/ST LEGER. Never mind his bumhole, pick him up.
OLD BEVIN. Tip 'un over cliff, thun, shall us? Over Cow Point
    where courtin' couple took tumble summer lass?
YOUNG BEVIN. Them weren't fust 'uns, either. An' there b'ain't
    no mark on 'un.
OLD BEVIN. Take 'us feet, thun.
YOUNG BEVIN (*lifting* DOWNCHILD'S *feet*). Tip where path
    slipped, right, pop?
OLD BEVIN (*moving off with their burden*). 'ead fuss, up an'
    over.
YOUNG BEVIN. 'ang about . . .

They go off. MOSCROP *stares into space. Suddenly* HEYDAY
enters, in a headscarf and raincoat.

HEYDAY. What's going on?
MOSCROP. Um.
HEYDAY. What's going on!
MOSCROP. Um.
HEYDAY. You were supposed to bring back Lucky. Lucky just
    ran past me.
MOSCROP. Um.
HEYDAY. Look, what is going on! (*Pause.* MOSCROP *looks very
    deliberately in the direction taken by the* BEVINS) What? (*He
    does the action again*) John, are you— (*He repeats it. She hurries
    away*)
MOSCROP. Not bothering with God now. Run His own fucking
    universe. **Not intervening any more.** (*Pause*)

Scene Two

The Manor. MOLLY *is knitting.* DOWNCHILD *is lying naked at her feet.*

DOWNCHILD. Got old man's blood now. Swift to bruise and slow to
    clot. Drop a ballet programme on my wrist, I come up blue. Can I
    get up?
MOLLY. I know all about age.
DOWNCHILD. Please?
MOLLY. I worked forty-five years. Know work, do you?
DOWNCHILD. Work?
MOLLY. Yes.
DOWNCHILD. No, I don't think I do.

MOLLY. Honest, anyway.

DOWNCHILD. Can I get up?

MOLLY. Six years Dolcis, stitcher, four years in the TMC, five years Vickers Armstrong, putting copper caps on shells, laid off come victory, five months on buses, seven years in liquorice allsorts, two in Kayser-Bondor, quality control, year in Smiths Electric, year in yo-yo packing, day shift hoola-hoops, four months in Tupperware, three years Dunlop Baby Carriages, upholstery—

DOWNCHILD. Battle honours of a mum—

MOLLY. Two years Mitsubishi, circuit-soldering, five night shifts and alternate Saturdays, five years canteen, ITT, five years canteen ITV. Time off in total, care to guess? Time off in forty years?

DOWNCHILD. No.

MOLLY. Two months for having baby. Two more for miscarriage. And two for hysterectomy. What a tiny cock you've got.

DOWNCHILD. I'm shy.

MOLLY. Makes no effort for a lady, eh?

DOWNCHILD. Let me sit up . . .

MOLLY. You look a wreck. The dirty life, is it? Posh parties? Posh disease? I worked for everythin' I eat, and I was always clean. Kept my baby lovely. Don't think I'll let you do it. 'ave 'er out of 'ere. Stick these needles in each eyeball first. Be warned.

DOWNCHILD (*sitting up*). Sorry, I must move. If you torture me to death I have to move. (SCADDING *enters, holding a bottle of whisky*)

SCADDING. The naughtiest old man in England.

DOWNCHILD. Oh, I don't know . . .

SCADDING. Enfants terribles I've heard of, but vieillards terribles? There's something wrong with that.

DOWNCHILD. I never cared too much for the idea of maturity. I hate maturity. Mature nations, mature writers, it's a con to rub the edge off a decent blade. (SCADDING *tosses a glass of whisky in* DOWNCHILD'S *face*)

SCADDING. Sorry. I wanted to do that.

DOWNCHILD. No, you go ahead.

SCADDING (*pouring another drink*). You don't look much undressed.

DOWNCHILD. That's why I have a tailor—(SCADDING *throws another glass over him*)

SCADDING. Dear, I've done it again.

DOWNCHILD. So you have—

SCADDING. **You make me childish! Aren't you ashamed?**

DOWNCHILD. I'll shut up.

SCADDING. Where's Ann?

MOLLY. Bath.

SCADDING. Still?

MOLLY. Yes.

SCADDING. Sign of nerves.

MOLLY. Yes.

SCADDING. Sign of dwindling confidence. Fetch her, will you?

(MOLLY *gets up, goes out*) Ann kept us waiting in cabinet. Made Shirley twitch. Made Shirley exercise her very crippled form of ridicule. Her indignation frothed up. Most unpleasant, made her spit. I said if we can be kept waiting months by foreign bankers it won't hurt to hang about ten minutes while an English secretary has a wash. Then Ann came down, smelling like a pine forest. Better whiff than Shirley, I might add. Stick that in your column. (*Pause. He gulps a drink*) I like a woman to have spotless underwear. (*Pause*) The joy of fumbling under clothes! Once had my fingers in her while Dennis argued passionately for shelling Reykjavik. Could make Ann catch her breath in mid-sentence. She had the best brain of the lot of them. Even half-coming she was quickest to the point. It's a big table in Downing Street. Hides a lot of creeping knees. (*He drinks the glass off*) I love her till it aches.

HEYDAY *comes in, smartly dressed. Pause.*

HEYDAY. I don't think I've ever seen a homosexual undressed.
DOWNCHILD. Then you must fuck with the light off. Half the men you slept with had a turn with me.
SCADDING. Ungrateful to be rude to Ann. Ann is your angel. Saved you from dropping off Cow Point. I don't know if in retrospect, that will be seen as senseless charity or not. She has a heart, you see, so much feeling she could spare a beast like you, who slashed her cheeks with filthy innuendo once. What a woman. Woman is a wonderful creature. Thank her, Tom.
DOWNCHILD. I do.
SCADDING. He is a gentleman. Of Eton, Oxford and the Shitshire Grenadiers.
HEYDAY. Give him his clothes.
SCADDING. No.
HEYDAY. Dress him, please.
SCADDING. Be witty, Tom.
HEYDAY. Leave him.
SCADDING. **Be a wit!**
DOWNCHILD. Comes better in a suit of clothes—
SCADDING. **No. Be witty naked.**
HEYDAY. Roy, you're—
SCADDING. **This is the man who pissed on us for seven years! This is the man who jeered at socialism in the columns of the capitalist press, who licked the bums of barons with his Fleet Street shit.** Be witty, Tom. (*He puts a foot on* DOWNCHILD'S *chest*) Wit! Wit!
DOWNCHILD. You're choking me—
SCADDING. **Amuse me, then.**
DOWNCHILD. Guy said to me—Guy Burgess this was—Guy who taught us love and Communism—who fucked a swathe through the Young Pioneers—Guy said to me in Moscow once—there are six hundred warheads aimed at England—every meadow has its

murder fixed—there will be no English to usher in another century
except the English who chose Moscow—I said that would be a very
brief reprieve for the race who created Shakespeare and the con-
centration camp as all our traitors put their seed in boys— (*He
bursts out in mock laughter*) I often think I should have stayed
in Moscow—would have got a dacha and a hamper sent from
Selfridges each month—

SCADDING. **More wit.**

DOWNCHILD. Trying—

SCADDING. **More wit.**

DOWNCHILD. I went to dinner with Frank Sydenham—Frank
Sydenham who chose to go with God—Fear God Frank we called
him—at the Café Royal—he had just come from visiting his
criminal—fresh from the guts of prison dripping guilt—and
ordered chicken Maryland in Beauvais sauce—and I said Frank
there's nothing like manslaughter to encourage chicken slaughter—
what you might call foul to fowl—

SCADDING. **More wit!**

DOWNCHILD. I was in a taxi with Nigel Nicholson—1950 this was—
Nigel had just lost his parliamentary seat—he was in a black mood—
clouds of misery he called them—but in French—Tom, he said,
Je souffre de me nuages de désespoir—I said frankly Nigel, if you
canvassed Croydon like a—

SCADDING (*pressing on his throat*). **Don't—know—French you—
snob—**

DOWNCHILD (*choking*). I can't—can't breathe—

SCADDING (*removing his foot*). If that's wit, I prefer Ken Dodd.

MOLLY (*entering*). Lana's 'ere. For Lucky.

SCADDING. Wednesday, is it? Time flies in the sticks.

HEYDAY. Send her up, then.

MOLLY *goes out.* DOWNCHILD *lies nursing his throat.*

SCADDING. Squire and peasant grappling in the afternoon . . .
the mad stuck in the ignorant . . . Tom, Ann and I surrender . . .
(*Pause.* DOWNCHILD *staggers upright, props himself against
a chair*) Now I'll tell you a witty story, Tom. (*Pause*) My very
good friend Lord Isted of Ramsgate, lately of Monaco, Brixton
and the Old Bailey, former chairman of the Saudi Football Club,
came up with a very sound idea. To Ann. Ann wanted a company,
you see. He said why didn't she set up an agency, building
factories in the assisted areas, claiming all the grants and subsidies.
It seemed a very good idea, in the spirit of our policies. Now here's
the funny bit. We needed a chairman. My very good friend Lord
Isted knew Lucky, Lord of Dicker.

HEYDAY. Lucky has family connections with an Irish bank.

SCADDING. At this time neither Frank nor I knew anything of Lucky's
homicidal tendencies.

HEYDAY. We called the companies after poets, starting with Auden.

My idea.

SCADDING. Got to Shelley, didn't we? The only thing was while we took
  the grants we got behind with putting up the factories . . .

HEYDAY. Then one night we got a phone call. From the call-box
  at the end of Downing Street.

SCADDING. Lucky's bloody fingers shovelling ten-pence pieces in.
  He had brained the nanny after a bad night down the club.
  Went blank, he says, then completely lucid, just as suddenly. He
  wanted protection.

HEYDAY. Or he'd spill the beans.

SCADDING. He got it. Now I call that a witty story, Tom. How's
  it end? (*Pause*)

DOWNCHILD. Dress me. (*Pause*) I'm not dressing myself. (*Pause*)
  Dress me!

(Clash of church bells and blackout)

Scene Three

The church. STOAT *enters with some tins of paint. He looks round him.*

STOAT. **The end of the world! Boom, you fuckers! Bring down the
  fuckin' slates!** (MOSCROP *appears, watches him*) **Russian rockets,
  burnin' out me eyes!** (*Left, the bells cease*)

MOSCROP. What do you want?

STOAT (*holding up the tins*). Repaint the saint. (MOSCROP *stares*)
  Two tins of Woolworth's Vinyl Silk. Saint Barry in the 'olocaust.
  The martyrin' of English youth. Geddit? Give us a ladder.

MOSCROP. Lord Cocky has commandeered the church—

STOAT. **Fuck 'im. Give us a ladder!** (*There is a commotion off*)
  geddit meself. (*He turns to leave*)

DOWNCHILD (*off*). **Be upstanding! Be upstanding in the court!**
  (*entering, followed by* HEYDAY *and* SCADDING). **The Holy
  Inquisition of Lord Cocky! See, his power comes!** Where d'you
  think you're going!

STOAT. Nowhere, Tom . . .

DOWNCHILD. Nowhere! He is going nowhere! In a single word,
  the story of his life! You are Exhibit A. Dumb monster. British
  youth. Put a label on yourself and do not leave the precincts
  of the court!

STOAT. Can't git up there with no ladder, can I?

DOWNCHILD. **Silence! Supreme old bugger in his moment of
  revenge! I dispense no justice, only persecute!** Where is my bed?
  I preside in horizontal posture, piles couchant, rectum demi-lax.
  (*He goes to the altar*)

MOSCROP. That is the altar.

DOWNCHILD. **Clear it! Today I am the only god!**

SCADDING. Clear it, John . . .

DOWNCHILD. Somebody make me a hat! A token of my power, a
symbol of my cruelty! **Stoat!** Fold up a newspaper, make me as
terrible as some farting pope! (STOAT *looks round, bewildered*)
Some old man rotting in the fundament but gorgeous of his
diamond knickers, shit smears on the rubies, sopping, pissy threads!
(MOSCROP *has cleared the altar table.* DOWNCHILD *mounts it*)
A Times if you can find one! I prefer my lies in English! I am going
to be unbearable today! (*He sees* MOSCROP *holding the crucifix*)
Away with that! All symbols of reconciliation out! (MOSCROP
starts to move off with the cross and altar cloth) I'll wear that!
MOSCROP. The cloth?
DOWNCHILD. The cloth, yes! Scuttling through the portals with
my costume, with my robe of office, drape me with it! Drape!
MOSCROP. It's—
SCADDING. Drape him, John.
DOWNCHILD (*as* MOSCROP *covers his shoulders*). Oh, I sink!
Like some dirty old bishop, sink under the weight! **Where's
my hat! My Biretta of divine newsprint! My mitre of untruth!**
(*He points to a spot*) Stand there. (MOSCROP *stands on the
spot*) Listen, the table groans . . . all the false oaths that have
been uttered here, to love, to cherish, to obey . . . the wood
must weep, it absorbs more lies than polish . . . **my hat!**
STOAT (*coming in with a conical paper hat*). Couldn't find no
Times. Vicar reads your paper.
DOWNCHILD. Then I will wear my gibberish. My own drivel
crown me with!
MOSCROP. Me?
DOWNCHILD. **You!** You're here to plead! Don't usurp the
cardinal's office! Stoat, put it on me, you unkind, unforgiving
boy, put on the crown of slander with your gentle murdering
hands . . . (STOAT *stands behind him, puts the paper hat on*)
Lovely. Show me a bishop could match his dignity. His leather.
His studs. What nobility!
STOAT. S'cockeyed.
DOWNCHILD. I love it that way. Like a trooper's beret,
tilted for a tart or a suck in a cubicle. I can spot the willing
by the angle of their caps. **Well, applaud me! I am saucy, aren't
I? Cheer!** (SCADDING *leads weak cheering*) Is that cheering?
(*He screws his finger in his ear comically*) That's not cheering!
(*They cheer again*) Better! Once again! (*They shout this time.
He stares at them*) God save me. God blind me to forgiveness.
God crush what little mercy existed in my soul. Amen.
(*Pause. He sits upright, expectantly*) I had thought of getting
in a jury, but they'd only acquit. **Step forward the accused!**
(SCADDING *and* HEYDAY *step forward*) Come on, get in
the dock!
SCADDING. Where—
DOWNCHILD. **There is the dock!**

SCADDING. Where—

DOWNCHILD. **There!** (*He indicates a particular place. They step into it. Pause*) Not enough. Where are the others? Where is **Andrew Roger Tudor Flannery Wills, Lord Dicker of Dicker in the County of Galway?**

SCADDING. Fucking.

DOWNCHILD. I accept that as due grounds for absence. His offence was trivial. What is murder against the charges I am bringing here today? Accuse yourselves, in order of grossness, vilest first. (*Pause.* DOWNCHILD *stares at the ceiling in feigned abstraction, like a judge*) Come on, don't hinder the proceedings! Only makes me weary and in consequence, vindictive! (*Pause*) Roy.

SCADDING. I aided and abetted a fugitive murderer to evade the law.

DOWNCHILD. My lord.

SCADDING. My lord.

DOWNCHILD. No, no! Your Holiness.

SCADDING. Your Holiness. (*Pause*)

DOWNCHILD. Try again.

SCADDING. Again?

DOWNCHILD. Yes. Plead again.

SCADDING. I was instrumental in obstructing the prosecution of a suspected murder. Your Holiness.

DOWNCHILD. Nope! (SCADDING *looks at* HEYDAY) **Don't look at her! I am the authority! Look at me!** (*Pause*)

SCADDING. I concealed the suspected criminal Lord Dicker out of personal consideration—

DOWNCHILD (*shaking his head*). Roy . . . Roy . . . (SCADDING *stops, irritated*) Roy . . . Roy . . . .

SCADDING. What! Sorry? What!

DOWNCHILD. **Do I detect a note of insubordination in your voice? Do I hear a little crossness, do I? The accused showing impatience with the judge? Never!**

SCADDING. No.

DOWNCHILD. Good. Now accuse yourself properly. The charges you are brought here for would not be listed by the courts. That is why I try you. **Plead.** (*Pause.* SCADDING *braces himself*)

SCADDING. I failed to report the appearance of a murder suspect on his appearance at the back door of 10, Downing Street on the night of—I dunno, what was it—(*He looks to* HEYDAY)

DOWNCHILD. Shh.

SCADDING. Ann, what was it?

DOWNCHILD. **Shhh!** (SCADDING *is silent*) I do not think—I do not honestly believe—he knows. (*Pause. He stands up, gathering the cope around him.* STOAT *appears with a ladder, puts it up against*

the tympanum. MOSCROP *looks aghast*) Imagine. (*Pause.
He creates*) The Commandant of Buchenwald, being taken,
being placed under the stare and spotlight of the assambled
judgement of the world, asked, do you plead guilty to your
crimes, says, in full and true contrition, yes, once I saw a
cigarette lighter slip from the pocket of a Jew as he was going to
the ovens, and I stooped and picked it up, and did not report
it but kept it for myself. This was a theft, and dishonourable. To
that I plead. (*Pause. He goes back to the table, lies on it*) Good!
That's good! Try again, Roy, in the light of my anecdote! (*Pause.
He shudders with joy*) Oh, I am a perfect judge! It suits me, does
it not absolutely suit me to wear authority like this! All my
cleverness brought me to this. And I am clever. I was always
clever. Real cleverness is so rare. They say Roy is clever, but there
is cleverness and cleverness. I have the latter.

MOSCROP. Roy . . . . he's painting out the tympan—

DOWNCHILD. **Do not refer to the prisoner! I am the Supreme
Pontiff of this place! Refer to me! Do I not carry on my head the
badge of my authority? Tremble! Tremble before the mirror!**
(MOSCROP *feigns trembling*) That isn't trembling. (*Pause*)
That is nothing like trembling. **This is trembling!** (*He shudders
violently*)

MOSCROP. It is trembling! That is a sixteenth-century masterpiece
by the Italian master Andrea del Marino. It's worth five hundred
thousand pounds!

DOWNCHILD (*sitting again*). I wonder what Andrea got for it? His
dinner and the hot breath of a sixteenth-century Devon tart, slagged
between the colours drying? I speak for Andrea. I am the artist.

MOSCROP. It is a work of art—

DOWNCHILD. **Don't talk to me about art! I know all about art.**
(*Pause*) Roy, plead. Plead better.

SCADDING. Apologia pro vita sua?

DOWNCHILD. Roy grasps. (*Pause*)

SCADDING. No.

DOWNCHILD. **Will not plead?**

SCADDING. No.

DOWNCHILD. Then I plead for him! (*He stands*) I gave boots to the
rotten to kick the healthy with.
I helped old women bleed in gutters.
I made young mothers take to drugs.
I stuffed despair through letter-boxes of the flats.
I made workmen in the factory ashamed of their beliefs.
I made them kiss my picture in the City.
I kicked hope out the hearts of men I didn't know.
I made a good thing fit for laughs.
I could have fucked History but I dribbled in my pants. (*Pause.
He sits*)
Something like that. I am poetic, obviously. (*Pause*)

SCADDING. No.

DOWNCHILD. **He denies the charges!** (*He stands up again*) **Introduce the exhibit!** (*He cups his hand to his mouth, as if voices were calling down corridors*) The Exhibit! The Ex–hib–it! **The exhibit–it!** (*Pause. He looks up at STOAT, painting on top of the ladder*) Oi. (STOAT *looks down*) You are the exhibit.

MOSCROP (*looking at the tympanum*). Oh, God Almighty . . . .

DOWNCHILD. Come down and stand before the court.

STOAT. Splash! Splash!

MOSCROP. Oh, God Almighty . . .

SCADDING. Steady, John . . .

DOWNCHILD. Down, you little Jesus. Get down here.

STOAT (*some way down the ladder*). Ain't so very bad, is it? I'm trained, yer see. 'ad lessons on remand. This tart came in a long dress, all wooden beads and 'air down to 'er arse crack. I painted tits. Nothin' but tits.

DOWNCHILD. Stand there. (STOAT *stands in the nave*)

STOAT. Like me?

DOWNCHILD (*sitting*). English boy.

STOAT. Like me?

DOWNCHILD. Circa 1970s. Under Scadding took first breath. The Scadding baby. Kiss him, Roy.

SCADDING. What.

DOWNCHILD. Kiss him. Now he's big. You kissed him when he was a strawberry wrinkle. I saw it. His shapeless mother shoved him underneath your gob, as if by politician's kiss came luck. Like touching hunchbacks. Thought your little lie might clear his eczema. Go on, kiss him, do! (SCADDING *forces himself forward*. STOAT *juts out a jaw*) Lovely! What a gorgeous reconciliation! Roy, you are the father of this boy.

STOAT. Is 'e? I'll be fucked!

DOWNCHILD. What's a father, but the man who makes you? If fathers were only donors of spoonfuls of spunk, we wouldn't love the word so much. No, he's your dad, he has a million children! And Lady Heyday, she's your mum . . . (*Pause*) Kiss him, mum . . . .

HEYDAY. No.

DOWNCHILD. Oh, but do! (*She looks at* SCADDING, *goes forward*) Her thin but subtle lips . . . (*She kisses* STOAT'S *cheek*)

STOAT (*Evilly*). Mouth

DOWNCHILD. No. She's not your mistress, she's your mum. Mouth's for passion, cheek's for gratitude. (*Pause. He looks at them, smiles benignly*) There . . . I do like that . . . !

HEYDAY. You are a vicious, evil thing.

DOWNCHILD. Call me a disease, why don't you?

HEYDAY. Yes.

DOWNCHILD. That clamps on your wet passages, and bursts out when you're ripe with sin . . .

STOAT. I like 'er. She does somethin' to me. I bet she's very clean . . .

(*He puts his hand up to her jacket*)
DOWNCHILD. No.
STOAT. Why not? 'ain't protestin'—
MOSCROP. **Stop that!** (*Pause*) Tell him to stop it or I'll knock
  him down. Flat on the flagstones. Tell him. (*Pause.* DOWNCHILD
  looks to STOAT)
DOWNCHILD. This work of art you may not touch. (*He looks at
  them, hops down again, walks round* STOAT) Of course I love
  him, this is my hypocrisy, this is my bad faith, isn't it, knowing
  he has blood on his boots, I needn't tell you what that does to me,
  being a gentle, Tunbridge Wells queer, only hot for nastiness, I
  tremble, I go stiff for murder, don't I, coming at the thought of
  old dears crashing on the kerbstone, black blood trickling out
  their lips **I should not be allowed to be like this!** (*Pause*)
  Acknowledge him. Acknowledge your creation. I give half a
  minute to the defence. (*He curls up on the table like a monkey*)
  And that's too generous. (STOAT *moves off*)
STOAT. Git on, all right? (*He scrambles up the ladder again*)
SCADDING. You were a parliamentary correspondent, Tom. (*Pause*)
  Is that half a minute? (*Pause*)
DOWNCHILD. **That's not a defence!**
SCADDING. No? I thought it was.
DOWNCHILD. **I want a defence! How can I adjudicate if there
  is no defence!**
SCADDING. God knows.
DOWNCHILD. Try again. (*He adopts a deliberate posture of
  attention*)
SCADDING. You were a parliamentary correspondent, Tom.
  (*Pause*) Meaning, you know how the beast moves.
DOWNCHILD. How does it move?
SCADDING. Not by skips. And not by jumps.
DOWNCHILD. How, then?
SCADDING. By twitches.
DOWNCHILD. Government by twitch! I know the thing you mean!
  And you were twitching England into socialism, were you, you were
  twitching Stoat out of his squalor!
SCADDING. I haven't finished yet.
DOWNCHILD. You have finished. I am a bastard of a judge, I won't
  indulge the prisoner! Who knows what horror you might come out
  with next, as if twitching weren't enough?
SCADDING. I never governed England, see?
DOWNCHILD. You didn't! You did not? Not govern England?
  What's this? Are you Scadding or aren't you? **Where's Scadding!
  Fetch Scadding! This is an imposter!** The penalty for impersonating
  a prime minister is to be believed!
SCADDING. I held office. I did not govern. (*Pause.* DOWNCHILD
  stares up at the roof)
DOWNCHILD. Who governed, then?

SCADDING. I was a baby, chucking bricks across the floor. On
Chequers carpets had my tantrums, on Downing Street tiles
piddled my despair. Banging my tiny fists against the **Real World**.
Do you know that phrase? It swung against me like a door, smack
in my baby kisser. The **Real World**. They trooped into my office,
civil servants, bankers, chiefs of police, and there it was, sat on
their shoulders grinning at me like an imp. Real World versus baby
tantrums. Heads of departments saying what I wanted wasn't on.
Their phrase—not on. Not in the Real World which they owned.
Sir This, Sir That, and Sir the Other. Ever wondered why I stuck
gangsters in the Honours List? My tantrum. My last revenge on all
the knights who grinned at me with marble teeth. And baby me,
who thought he drank of power. Out of the baby feeder of
Westminster, guzzling air. Never. Never touched the shit that
hung off power's arse. (*Pause*) All the muck you wrote about me,
all the dirty newsprint flung at Ann—pissing on a baby, Tom.
Never touched the real dirt, did you? (*Pause*) Defence rests.
DOWNCHILD. Good speech! Good speech! (*He shouts up to* STOAT)
Did you hear that! Lovely bit of apologia! Gorgeous! Gorgeous!
But I wonder if I missed a bit? No shame, was there? Or did I miss
it? I do love shame, awful thirst for it, can you see it, vicar? Roy's
shame? Slipped down a grating, did it? **Is the shame there, vicar?
Look for it!** (MOSCROP *is bewildered*) **Get on your knees and look
for it!** (*He gets down*) As if the spectacle of Stoat was not enough
to make us shudder, Stoat who could not scratch his name until
I met him, who was more ignorant than a black boy in the bush—
STOAT. **Could write my name!**
DOWNCHILD. Write, yes, but spell it? (*He turns to* MOSCROP) Have
you found it, vicar? Have you found Roy's shame?
SCADDING. I have none.
DOWNCHILD. **None!** None, he says? (*Pause*) Stoat, he is not stung
by you, by your foul beauty, not touched! **Have you no soul,
mean father!**
HEYDAY. What did you want, then? Blood in the streets? (*Pause*)
DOWNCHILD. Oh, yes. Blood, yes. Have always wanted blood. Old
as I am, I welcome it. Because there's blood already. Blood on
the landings. Blood on the stairs. Ask my slim killer, is there blood?
Blood, yes, although it makes me faint.
SCADDING. His blood it would have been. (*He indicates* STOAT)
Shot out from underneath a tank.
DOWNCHILD. The Real World?
SCADDING. Would have fired rockets in the flats. I saw that written
in the marble teeth. Sir This, Sir That, and Sir the Other. Their
silver partings whispered tanks. I never sat with bankers but their
teeth clicked tanks. I was a very clever baby, Tom. Preferred
delinquents to dead boys. (*Pause*)
DOWNCHILD. Guy said to me, delicious Guy, don't worry, England
won't go bang, you'll always find a restaurant open somewhere,

Tom, it will rot down like a marrow, collapsing inwards, like a
corpse, no sound but little hiss of gases, organ flop on organ,
jelly shudders, spills into a rancid juice . . . . I could not have
chosen a better time to live, could I? I am at one with my age, I
am the Zeitgeist, fucking cold and dead within . . . (*Pause*)
Scadding, I find you guilty of humanity. Obviously you cared
too much for Stoat, and to spare him pain, delivered him into
the compost. **Next!** (*He stands*) **I call The Queen of England to the
stand!** The Queen of England? No, not the parched-skin hag who
never has enough chairs for a garden-party, the real queen, the
proper monarch, you—(*He points to* HEYDAY) tell us, did you
practise with a novel on your head to walk so straight, glide along
as if inanimate? **Don't splash paint on the magistrate!**

SCADDING (*to* HEYDAY). Don't speak if you don't want to.

DOWNCHILD. What's this! You are not to interfere with her, however
hard you find it! Keep your fingers locked in one another, tie them
down, she will not have them in her knickers, burrowing like
hamsters, will you miss? **Give your full name.**

HEYDAY. Ann Joy Coote.

DOWNCHILD. Beautiful! The sheer simplicity of it! Three syllables!
Mine is—shall I tell you? What I have never uttered to another, not
even in the heat of swopping truths? I will! Today's a special day!
Off, everything! Strip! Strip! **Ernest!** (*He squeals*) There!
Broadbent! (*He squeals again*) Ernest Broadbent! (*He waves an
arm*) Now forget it, I command you! Have you forgotten it?

HEYDAY. Yes.

DOWNCHILD (*sitting*). I was taking evidence. Do you plead guilty?

HEYDAY. Yes.

DOWNCHILD. To what?

HEYDAY. Sin.

SCADDING. Ann—

HEYDAY. I want to—

SCADDING. Yes, but—

DOWNCHILD. Sin, she said.

SCADDING. **He ain't no fucking priest.**

DOWNCHILD (*standing*). **I am! I am not a priest? I am! I am the High
Priest of Gossip!** Lay your sins before me and I'll make proper prose
of them. What are your sins, dear? Tell me, who was it climbed the
lovely valley of your arse and—

STOAT. **Dirt-ty! Being dir-ty!**

DOWNCHILD. **Silence up there! I am a priest, aren't I?** (*He turns to*
HEYDAY) Where were we?

SCADDING. Not to him, Ann.

HEYDAY. Why not?

SCADDING. Because he hates you.

HEYDAY. Good.

SCADDING. We don't have to do this!

DOWNCHILD. Oh, you do! You do! Or this goes to my editor, and simultaneously to the DPP! (*Pause*)

SCADDING. Hate to see her—

DOWNCHILD. Yes, of course—

SCADDING. When I love every—

DOWNCHILD. Yes, indeed—

SCADDING. Ann, even plunging headlong down the well, grasp at the moss, snatch till you're dead, eh? That's how we came through.

HEYDAY. Yes.

SCADDING. Dignity. Dignity, please. (*Pause*)

HEYDAY. I've sinned against myself.

SCADDING. Oh, fuck!

DOWNCHILD. **Contempt! Contempt!**

SCADDING. Not this, for Christ's sake—

DOWNCHILD. **Stop this! I will have to clear the court!**

STOAT. **Dir-ty! Dir-ty!**

DOWNCHILD (*standing*). **Cut that out, monster!**

STOAT. **Boll-ocks!**

DOWNCHILD (*to* MOSCROP). Command silence! Discipline the Court!

MOSCROP. Silence.

DOWNCHILD. **Discipline it!**

MOSCROP. **Sil-ence in Lord Coc-ky's court!** (*Pause.* DOWNCHILD *smiles, sits*)

DOWNCHILD. Good. (*He looks to* HEYDAY) Yes?

HEYDAY. What I had to do, to triumph. Be dolly on the one hand, giving off the proper smells, well-shaved and shiny, petal calves, underarms like silk for alcoholic tongues to lick, and on the other, brute male sense, to spot an opportunity, to wring it out. Dared not spill my little bit of pity. My female something, crushed it dead.

SCADDING. Your female something was alive and well, Ann, when I knew it.

HEYDAY. Where? Around your cock?

SCADDING. **You wanted power! Said so, didn't you!**

HEYDAY. I did.

SCADDING. Well, then!

HEYDAY. Had to murder so much of myself.

SCADDING. We all do! It's called politics!

HEYDAY. In 1960, I had three General Secretaries on the beach . . .

SCADDING (*still looking at* MOSCROP). Well, you were good at it, weren't you? You liked it once. Might still, for all I know . . .

HEYDAY. I made myself.

SCADDING. Can't make yourself.

HEYDAY. Forced it.

SCADDING. Never! (*Pause*) Men read you. Read her, don't they, John? Pulled 'em 'cos you liked it.

HEYDAY. He has to know me better than I know myself.

SCADDING. **Oh, yes!** (*Pause*) Sorry. (*Pause*) Can't bear to hear you say all we did was against your will . . .

DOWNCHILD. All this self-accusation spoils my appetite! How can I
prosecute? I shall be moved to pity by the lady's relentless vanity.
Who can resist her? Pity! Pity! Pity! Stamp on it! (*He stamps his
feet*) **Get off!** (*He stamps again*) All right, you may proceed . . .

HEYDAY. I wanted power. Wanted it even more than Roy. And
when it came, did not know what to do with it. The thing, I thought,
was getting my bum on the chair. Not true. The fish-eyed Tory
never wonders why he's there. He knows. To serve the baying and
the booming class. But me? For my pushy mother, was it? Why?

DOWNCHILD. She pleads well, Roy. Better than you.

SCADDING. Sea air. On top of menopause.

HEYDAY. **Shut up!**

MOSCROP. Yes, Roy—

SCADDING (*savagely*). Yes, Roy?

HEYDAY. Help me!

DOWNCHILD. I will. (*Pause*) Because I am the great Judge Crab. I
should be the Lord Chief Justice of all England, I should wear
his seedy plush, flung on my carapace. The greatest judge, you see,
is he who has lived on the bottom, who has breathed the bottom,
eaten bottom, who is made of bottomness, like me. What Old
Bailey bugger could ever feel you like I do? Like a tapeworm stick
my head out of your mouth and speak your life, nourished of
your dinner, hook somewhere far down in your bowel? No, I am
the expert. Only sinners for magistrates! Empty the gaols to get
a decent bench! (*Pause*) I know why you sat in Downing Street,
and so do you. You did it out of hate. To giggle naked in the
shadow of the cenotaph, to have your gender sucked while buses
tore along Whitehall, packed with workers swaying on the upper
deck, going where you came from, down to the rusty, rattling
docks. Sinning the mighty sin. Doing the great contempt. **I know
it! I know it, oh, I know it, all because you got no love!**
(STOAT *comes down the ladder, looks at* DOWNCHILD)

STOAT. Done it. (DOWNCHILD *is staring, fixed*) My English
boy in flames. (*Pause*) Done it. (*He points up at the tympanum*)
Tha's me. I look up, the flash of disintegrating cities in my eye.
One 'and lies on my crutch, symbol of male modesty, the other,
not so well painted, grasps dictionaries, symbol of futile
communication. Beneath me feet lie melted motors and the
junky glitter of a mechanistic age. In the background is a riot,
burnin' goals. Front right, a sensitive policeman weeps, and
prays—vainly—for peace. (*He takes a final glance at his work*)
Ta ta. I'm off.

DOWNCHILD. Off where?

STOAT. London. Big sweat. Big dust.

DOWNCHILD. Not yet, Barry. Have a seat.

STOAT. Must go. I'm 'itching, see?

DOWNCHILD. Hitching? Why are you hitching? Don't you like

the car?

STOAT. No.

DOWNCHILD. Why not? (STOAT *starts to leave.* DOWNCHILD *stands up*) **The court is not yet risen! No one move!** (STOAT *stops, looks back*) Come here. (*He goes to leave again*) **Look, I'm God, aren't I? Because I'm literate!** (*Pause*) Teach you words, don't I?

STOAT. Fuck words. Picture's best.

DOWNCHILD. This is for you, Barry.

STOAT. Barry, now?

DOWNCHILD. So you may see. To give you eyes.

STOAT. Got eyes.

DOWNCHILD. **To see through this.** (*He points to* HEYDAY *and* SCADDING. *Pause*)

STOAT. So 'e's a gangster. So she's a tart. So the world's bent. 'ow about that!

DOWNCHILD. **Well, resist it!** (*Pause.* STOAT *looks at him*) Please . . . (*Pause*)

STOAT. Off to breathe the big lights, Tom. Swaller Leicester Square an' spew it up again . . .

DOWNCHILD. Dignity, Barry. Got to find a little bit . . .

STOAT. **Dignity! Me!** (*He stares at* DOWNCHILD) Me with my funny 'ip? Prancin' on the corner of the block? Dignity? Never would 'ave fucked me if I'd 'ad that. (*He casts a glance at the tympanum, looks to* MOSCROP) You wanna thank me. Ain't gonna be no foreigners queuing to look at that. (*He goes out. Pause*)

DOWNCHILD. I thought, when I began my column, when I invented Cocky's Window on the World, to put two squalors side by side. I thought if in column one I showed the dribble and the spillage of a debutante, and nudged it up against the death of infants in a Glasgow slum, I'd touch some dim mechanism in the English mind, trigger something that was curled up in the dark, justice, perhaps, that had dried up and shrivelled like a nut. I was so quick and smart, thinking I could twist the tail of the Canadian dwarf, and make his Daily Liar spill a bit of anger on the bus. But no. They read the one, they read the other, wept in one, felt envy in the other. **Saw no discrepancy.** It was me got done . . . .

LANA *and* YOUNG BEVIN *appear in the door.*

YOUNG BEVIN. Sumthin' to tell 'ee. Ol' barmy what she cuddles with's gone shot 'unself. (*Shocked silence.* LANA *lets out a wail*)

HEYDAY. Lucky?

YOUNG BEVIN. When she was puttin' on 'er knickers. Cums this bluddy bang. T'is nutter's brains all over 'er . . .

SCADDING. Too late. Like everything that Lucky did.

HEYDAY (*to* BEVIN). Go home. And wait. (*He starts to lead her out, stops*)

YOUNG BEVIN. Ca 'ave abortion, now, orl right?

DOWNCHILD. No. (BEVIN *stares at* DOWNCHILD) I'll buy it off
you.
YOUNG BEVIN. Buy baby?
DOWNCHILD. How much do you want for it? (*Pause. He calculates*)
YOUNG BEVIN. 'S'nart or'nary baby, is it? S'gart posh blud in't.
DOWNCHILD. Quite. How much?
YOUNG BEVIN. 'S'll want 'undred at the least . . .
DOWNCHILD. Fifty.
YOUNG BEVIN. Fifty! S'bin sick for all o' three months, a'n't thee?
(LANA *nods*)
LANA. Terrible.
DOWNCHILD. Fifty down. Fifty on delivery. My final offer.
YOUNG BEVIN. Dun!

DOWNCHILD *takes out his wallet, gives the money to* LANA.
She turns to go.

DOWNCHILD. Just a minute. (*He kneels, kisses her belly*) Put my
seal on it.

He gets up. BEVIN *turns to lead* LANA *out.* BEVIN *looks at him.*
Sound of seas crashing.

Scene Four

The field. A wild sea below. SCADDING, HEYDAY, MOLLY, MOSCROP,
THE BEVINS *and* LANA, *dressed darkly, stand patiently in a group.*
LANA *holds her baby in a shawl. They have been here a long time. At
last a car door slams, and* DOWNCHILD *appears, smart and correct, a
flower in his buttonhole. He stops, looks at them all. Then he goes to*
LANA, *and takes the baby from her. He looks at it, holds it out to*
MOSCROP.

DOWNCHILD. Christen it.
MOSCROP. What?
DOWNCHILD. Never mind the name. Just christen it. (MOSCROP
looks pained) Leave a blank. I'll fill the name in later. (MOSCROP
takes the baby. DOWNCHILD *wanders to* SCADDING)
MOSCROP. We are gathered together in the sight of the Lord our God
and in the—
DOWNCHILD. Too loud. (MOSCROP *stops, then murmurs*) Been
thinking, Roy.
SCADDING. Yes.
DOWNCHILD. How you'd be headlines for a fortnight. But then how
you'd slip, down to second leader. Then off the front page altogether,
bob up somewhere on page three, then seep away in little paragraphs
to be forgot, become a little fragment in the dirty tapestry of public
life, bore us with your memoirs—
SCADDING. I don't know that—

DOWNCHILD (*wagging a finger*). Oh, yes, you would! I know you
   would! In the Open Prison library, scratch your defence. (*Pause.
   He looks at him*) No. Mustn't let your horror spill away in news.
   Kill news. Or we will never have a decent newspaper. (*He turns*)
   Have you done yet, vicar? (SCADDING *looks to* HEYDAY)
SCADDING. Grasp at the moss, eh? Ann, we're through . . . . !
MOSCROP. Nomine patri, filii—
DOWNCHILD. No, I don't like that—
MOSCROP. Et spiritu sanctu—
DOWNCHILD. **I don't like that!** (MOSCROP *stops.* DOWNCHILD
   holds out his arms for the baby. MOSCROP *gives it to him. He
   looks at it*) She will be mad, won't she? (*Suddenly he hoists the
   baby in the air*) **In madness I christen you! Immerse you in the
   sea!** (*He holds the baby over the edge of the cliff*)
LANA. **Don't drop 'un! Don' drop 'un over!**
YOUNG BEVIN. **Christ!**
DOWNCHILD. **Why not! I own it, don't I?**
HEYDAY. Put it down!
DOWNCHILD. **Save it, can't I? Save it from our English mess!**
HEYDAY. Don't let it go! Don't let it—
DOWNCHILD. Life of squalor on our barmy rock!
OLD BEVIN. Oh, you loony bugger!
LANA. **He–lp!**
DOWNCHILD. **Shuddup!** (*Pause*) Roy speak. Roy. Give us a
   reason why it ought to live. What lies before it. Paint its future.
   (*Pause.* SCADDING *doesn't move.* DOWNCHILD *goes nearer the
   edge*) **Give us a reason, Roy, will you!**
HEYDAY (*as* SCADDING *doesn't speak*). If someone has to go,
   I will!
DOWNCHILD. No, no! I'm tired of your old sin! Death's for the
   innocent. **Last chance,** Roy. Argue it. (LANA *screams, tries to
   rush at* DOWNCHILD, *but* BEVIN *holds her*) Oh, Roy! It's
   cruelty! Say something! (SCADDING *is still*) He can't . . . (*He
   looks at the baby*) He can't, you see . . . give.you one whisper
   why you should persevere . . . (*he shrugs*) Quit Roy's world now,
   then. What baby with an ounce of sense would choose to struggle
   in Roy's desert?

*He chucks the baby off the cliff, almost casually. There is a chorus
of screams.* DOWNCHILD *falls to his knees and tries to protect his
face.*

OLD BEVIN. Murder 'un!
MOLLY. Kill 'im! Kill 'im!
YOUNG BEVIN. Over with 'un!

They launch themselves at him. SCADDING *slowly falls to his knees.
His shoulders heave. He weeps.* DOWNCHILD *is dragged to the edge of
the cliff.*

MOLLY. Over with 'im!

STOAT *appears, holding the baby.*

STOAT. Oi.
OLD BEVIN. Git over, thou clingin' cunt!
STOAT. **Oi.**

They turn. LANA *screams with ecstasy, rushes to the baby. They stop.*
DOWNCHILD'S *nose is bleeding.*

DOWNCHILD. Is that quick, Stoat? So I know next time. Do you call
   that quick?
STOAT. You were too far over. I nearly dropped the fucking thing . . .
OLD BEVIN. Get out us place now, tha' cocky bugger, as fast as shit,
   or I'll stick more creases on ol' sinner's mush o' thine.
DOWNCHILD. I made an English politician cry! Have you no love of
   spectacle? Bevin, it's worth a box of babies! In forty years of
   calumny I never drew a decent tear like that. (*He goes to* SCADDING)
   The dreamers, they are always crying, but this, who never dreamed . . .
   (*He puts a finger to* SCADDING'S *cheek, licks it*) It's salt! I do
   declare it's salt, not piss!
HEYDAY. You are an unkind man. I don't think you will die with any
   grace.
DOWNCHILD. No. I shan't recall my sins, and suck them. Lick my
   misdemeanours in the panic of senility. Never, while there are
   sweeter things to put my lips around . . . (*He goes closer to her*) No
   dignity. No wisdom. Serenity. Or peace. Kick to the finish!

She turns, goes off. MOLLY, MOSCROP, THE BEVINS *follow her.*
SCADDING *gets to his feet, looks at him.*

SCADDING. Come to the house and wash.
DOWNCHILD. Thanks, Roy, I like to wear my blood.
SCADDING. Your nose is all—
DOWNCHILD. My wound stripes, Roy. I wouldn't swill them down a
   sink. In Fleet Street tomorrow I shall sit there, caked, and they will
   know I had a story, and wonder what became of it . . . .
   (SCADDING *goes out.* DOWNCHILD *turns to* STOAT) Home,
   Stoat! Drive on the wrong side of the line, whoop our way through
   stagnant villages! (*They start to go off.* DOWNCHILD *stops*) Christ.
   Give us an arm. Something's gone in my gut. (*He forces a smile*)
   Colitis, complicated by a sharp attack of rural boots . . . (*They
   start. He falls*) Christ, why am I on my knees?
STOAT (*horrified*). I'll get 'em back—I'll call 'em—Oi!
DOWNCHILD. I'll drive—you bite my neck—whisper me your
   catalogue of terrors—
STOAT. Tom—your gob—
DOWNCHILD. Swallow me at traffic lights—make long lines of
   nagging husbands hoot!
STOAT. Tom—you're bleeding from the gob—

DOWNCHILD. They call it passion, silly boy— (STOAT *takes a step backwards*) Oh, don't be offended—come on—don't—don't tell me You're squeamish, Jesus Christ—after vour apprenticeship, don't— (STOAT *lets out a cry of horror*)—**Stoat, it's only blood . . . .** (STOAT *runs off, calling after the others*) Guy? Guy? Is that you? Touch me from your little grave in Moscow? Poke a flabby finger through the snow? Soviet Y-Fronts bulging with distress. Did right, didn't we?

Blackout